Public Speaking

Custom Edition for Babson College
RHT 1300 Course Materials

Michael Osborn
Suzanne Osborn
Randall Osborn

Taken from:
Public Speaking, Eighth Edition
by Michael Osborn, Suzanne Osborn, and Randall Osborn

Custom Publishing

New York   Boston   San Francisco
London   Toronto   Sydney   Tokyo   Singapore   Madrid
Mexico City   Munich   Paris   Cape Town   Hong Kong   Montreal

Cover Art: Illustration by Renee Sartell

Taken from:

Public Speaking, Eighth Edition
by Michael Osborn, Suzanne Osborn, and Randall Osborn
Copyright © 2009 by Pearson Education, Inc.
Published by Allyn & Bacon
Boston, Massachusetts 02116

The special edition published in cooperation with Pearson Custom Publishing.

Printed in the United States of America

10 9 8

2009240090

LR

**Pearson
Custom Publishing**
is a division of

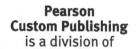

www.pearsonhighered.com

ISBN 10: 0-558-30608-X
ISBN 13: 978-0-558-30608-3

Contents

15 Persuasion and Argument   368

Selected Chapters from
Public Speaking
Eighth Edition

Michael Osborn, Suzanne Osborn,
and Randall Osborn

Structuring Your Speech

This chapter will help you

- develop a simple, balanced, and orderly speech design
- select and arrange your main points
- plan transitions to make your speech flow smoothly
- prepare effective introductions and conclusions for your speeches

Every discourse ought to be a living creature; having a body of its own and head and feet; there should be a middle, beginning, and end, adapted to one another and to the whole.

—Plato

Suppose you must take a course in physics next semester, and you get the following evaluations from RateMyProfessors.com of the two instructors scheduled to teach the course:

JOHNSON, DENNIS: Professor Johnson is really cool. He tells a lot of funny stories and his lectures are always entertaining. But he doesn't explain difficult material in any systematic fashion, so it's hard to take notes. When it's time for departmental examinations, you often don't know how or what to study.

MARTINEZ, MARIA: Professor Martinez is very businesslike when explaining her expectations for class assignments. She starts each lecture by reviewing the material covered in the last session and asks if anyone has questions. Her lectures are easy to follow. She points out what is most important for students to know and uses clear examples that make difficult ideas easier to understand and apply.

Which instructor would you choose? If you care about your education, chances are you'd choose Professor Martinez. Everyone likes to be entertained, but most people prefer well-organized speakers when the message is important. Indeed, studies suggest that students learn more from instructors who are well focused and businesslike, and they generally dislike instructors who persistently go off on tangents, jump from one idea to another, ramble, or are generally disorganized.[1]

This preference highlights the importance of structure and organization for effective public speaking. Presenting well-organized speeches helps listeners to follow, understand, and remember your message. Being well organized also enhances audience perceptions of your credibility and helps you cope with communication apprehension. The better prepared you are, the less anxious you will feel.

In this chapter, we discuss some principles and offer advice to help you structure speeches that will be readily understood, compelling, and easily remembered. We begin with the basic principles underlying "good form." Then we offer some practical advice concerning how to develop the body of your speech, how to add transitions to make your speech flow smoothly, and how to prepare effective introductions and conclusions.

Principles of Good Form

The principles of good form for effective speech organization reflect the way that people, either by nature or custom, tend to arrange and make sense of ideas and information. To develop good form, you should keep your presentations simple, balance the parts of your speeches, and arrange your main points so that they develop in a meaningful pattern. In short, good form depends on simplicity, balance, and order.

Simplicity

A simple design makes it easy for listeners to follow, understand, and remember your message.[2] To achieve **simplicity** in your speeches, you should limit the number of your main ideas, repeat them for emphasis, and keep your wording direct and to the point.

Number of Main Points. The fewer main points in a speech, the better, because each main point must be developed with supporting material. It takes time to present information, examples, narratives, and testimony effectively. Short speeches like those you will present in class should rarely have more than three main points. Consider what happens when a speech becomes overburdened with main points:

Thesis statement:	Our approach to welfare does not work.
Main points:	I. There are too many programs.
	II. The programs often duplicate coverage.
	III. Some people who need help are left out.
	IV. The programs are poorly funded.
	V. The programs waste money.
	VI. Recipients have no input into what is needed.
	VII. The programs create dependence.
	VIII. The programs stifle initiative.
	IX. The programs rob the poor of self-respect.

Each of these points may be important, but presented this way, they could be confusing. It would be hard for listeners to remember them because they are not organized in a meaningful way. Let's see how these ideas might be clustered into a simpler structural pattern:

Thesis statement:	Our approach to welfare does not work.
Main point:	I. Our approach does not work because it is inadequate.
Subpoints:	A. We don't fund it sufficiently.
	B. Some people who need help get left out.
Main point:	II. Our approach does not work because it is inefficient.
Subpoints:	A. There are too many programs.
	B. There is too much duplication.
	C. There is too much waste of money.
Main point:	III. Our approach does not work because it is insensitive.
Subpoints:	A. It creates dependence.
	B. It stifles initiative.
	C. It robs people of self-respect.

This simple structure makes the speech easier to follow. The thesis statement offers an overview of the message. Each main point elaborates and develops the thesis statement. The subpoints organize and focus the secondary ideas so that they support the major ideas. Overlapping ideas have been combined, and unnecessary ideas have been omitted. The new structure answers the questions raised in the minds of

simplicity   Suggests that a speech has a limited number of main points and that they are short and direct.

A well-organized speech is easy to follow.

thoughtful listeners in response to the thesis statement: *Why isn't our approach to welfare working?* The overall result is a design that satisfies such listeners and helps them remember what they have heard.

Repeating Key Points for Emphasis.   Repeating key ideas and information is a time-honored strategy of simplifying the structure of a speech. Consider the revised example. The central message that "our approach to welfare does not work" is reinforced by repeating that point while discussing each of the system's shortcomings. Strategic repetition is such a powerful tool for simplifying speeches that it has been built into the standard speaking format in which speakers preview their messages in the introduction, develop them in the body of the speech, and then review them in the conclusion. Strategic repetition is summed up in the following adage:

- Tell them what you're going to tell them.
- Tell them.
- Tell them what you told them.

Phrasing Main Points.   You should state your main points as simply as possible for easy understanding and retention. The ability to state your major ideas and present information in simple, direct statements is crucial to developing your communication skills. Again, consider our revised example. Not only has the wording been simplified, but the use of the same word pattern to introduce each main point makes for a message that is easy to understand. The repeated phrase "Our approach does not work because it is" suggests that these are the main points and makes them easy to remember. It further helps the differences to stand out as the speaker refers to the "Three I's" of welfare (inadequacy, inefficiency, and insensitivity). We further discuss the use of the parallel construction of main points in Chapter 10.

Balance

Balance means that the major parts of your speech—the introduction, the body, and the conclusion—receive appropriate development. Instructors generally specify time limits for speeches, so keep these in mind as you plan your message. It can be very upsetting to finish the first main point of your speech and find that you have only one minute left and two more main points plus your conclusion to present. Time yourself as you practice your speech to be sure it fits within the time limits. The following suggestions will help you plan a balanced presentation:

1. *The body should be the longest part of your speech.* It contains your major ideas. If you spend three minutes on your introduction, a minute and a half on the body, and thirty seconds on the conclusion, your speech will be out of balance.

2. *Balance the development of each main point.* If your main points seem equally important, you should give each point *equal emphasis*. This strategy might be appropriate for the speech on the Three I's of welfare policy, in which each point merits equal attention. If your main points differ in importance, you might start

balance   Suggests that the introduction, body, and conclusion receive their proper share of the time allotted for the speech.

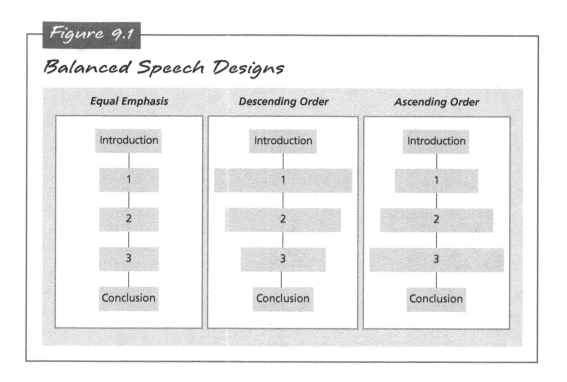

Figure 9.1

Balanced Speech Designs

with the most important point, spending the most time on it, and then present the other points with a *descending* emphasis, according to their importance. For example, in a speech that follows the problem–solution design, you may need to convince listeners first that there actually is a problem. Thus, you should devote most of your time to establishing this first point. Alternatively, you might wish to develop your main points with an *ascending* emphasis. If listeners agree there is a problem but don't know what to do about it, then you should devote most of your time to your solution, the second main point. Figure 9.1 illustrates these variations of emphasis.

3. *The introduction and conclusion should be approximately equal in length.* Your introduction may be slightly longer than your conclusion, but the total amount of time spent on your introduction and conclusion should be less than the amount spent on the body of your speech. As a general rule, in a five-minute presentation, the combined length of the introduction and conclusion should last about a minute. This leaves four minutes to develop the main points of the message.

Order

Order in a speech requires a consistent pattern of development from beginning to end. A well-ordered speech starts by introducing its subject and purpose, continues by developing the main ideas in the body of the speech, and ends by summarizing and reflecting on the meaning of what has been said. To build an orderly speech, you should follow the advice implied by Plato in our chapter-opening epigram: Design the body of the speech first, because that is where you will do the work of presenting, illustrating, and proving your message. Once you have structured the body of your speech, you can prepare an introduction and a conclusion that are custom-tailored for your message.

order   A consistent pattern used to develop a speech.

Structuring the Body of Your Speech

 he body of your speech should highlight your main points and develop them effectively. The process of structuring the body of your speech includes selecting, arranging, and supporting your main points.

Selecting Your Main Points

The **main points** are the most important ideas of your message, the points that fulfill your specific purpose. As you research your topic, you should discover some repeated themes. These are the most important issues connected with your topic. Consider how they relate to your specific purpose, your thesis statement, and the needs and interests of your listeners. Your main points will come from these repeated themes and your analysis of their relevance.

Let's look at how you might select the main points for a speech on global warming. Begin by preparing a **research overview**, listing your main sources of information and a summary of the major ideas from each. Figure 9.2 presents a sample research overview based on four sources of information: a *Time* magazine special issue, summary reports from the Intergovernmental Panel on Climate Change, an article from *U.S. News & World Report*, and research reports from the Environment News Service. Scanning the overview, you might come up with the following repeated themes:

- Increased temperatures are evidence of global warming.
- Human activities cause global warming.
- Global warming will cause climate changes.
- Global warming will cause health, environmental, and economic problems.

Once you have identified the main themes from the research, you should determine how they relate to your specific purpose and your audience. In this example, let us assume that your specific purpose is "to inform my audience about the problem of global warming." You anticipate that the audience's knowledge of the subject may be limited and possibly even confused. Therefore, you decide that your first major challenge is to define global warming in terms these listeners can understand,

Figure 9.2

Sample Research Overview

Environment News Service	Time	U.S. News	Intergovernmental Panel on Climate Change
1. Increase in Earth's temperature	1. Use less energy	1. CO_2 problems	1. Climate changes
2. Build-up of greenhouse gases	2. Drive efficient vehicles	2. Climate changes	2. U.S. largest polluter
3. Flooding and climate changes	3. Go with solar or gas energy	3. What we can do A. Learn more about it B. Save energy C. Drive less	3. Energy and global warming
4. Attributed to human influences	4. Geoengineering ideas		4. Transportation and global warming

main points The most prominent ideas of the speaker's message.

research overview A listing of the main sources of information that could be used in a speech and of the major ideas from each source.

using simple language, everyday comparisons, and clear explanations. After that, you want to increase your audience's understanding of the causes and potential effects of global warming. In light of the repeated themes you identified in your research overview, you might come up with the following main points:

1. Global warming is a gradual warming of the earth's surface.

2. Humans are contributing to global warming through industrial emissions, environmental destruction, and personal energy use.

3. Global warming may cause severe climate changes and health problems.

Arranging Your Main Points

Once you have decided on your main points, you should arrange them using a design that is appropriate for your audience, fits your material, and serves your specific purpose. As noted earlier in this chapter, people organize ideas and information into patterns that are easy to comprehend and remember. These patterns serve as templates through which we perceive and experience the world. They set up expectations for processing incoming information. The way you arrange material in your speeches should be in harmony with these expectations. The major designs for organizing brief presentations are categorical, comparative, spatial, sequential, chronological, causation, problem–solution, refutative, and narrative.

Categorical. A categorical design arranges the main ideas of a speech in terms of natural or customary divisions. For instance, speakers addressing the "three causes of global warming" or "three strategies to avoid paying excessive taxes" would probably arrange their main ideas in a categorical design. Categories are useful for arranging large amounts of information, and they reflect our basic tendency to group bits of information on the basis of their perceived similarity.

Comparative. A comparative design begins with determining the similarities or differences between things, events, and ideas. For instance, an informative speaker might compare the San Andreas and New Madrid fault zones in terms of the frequency and severity of major earthquakes. Similarly, persuasive speakers might compare the Republican Party and Democratic Party positions on important issues. Speakers often try to explain the meaning of current events by comparing them with similar events in the past. For example, opponents of our military involvement in Iraq often invoke comparisons to the conflict in Vietnam. Comparative speeches are especially useful for topics that are new or difficult for audience members to understand.

Spatial. A spatial design arranges the main points as they occur in physical space, often taking listeners on an orderly, imaginary tour. For example, if you were asked to give a group of incoming freshmen a tour of your school library, you might use a floor plan as a presentation aid as you lead them through a guided tour of the different departments of the library where they can access reference materials, periodicals, local applications, and so on. An effective spatial design provides your audience with a verbal map.

Sequential. A sequential design explains the steps of a process in the order in which they should be taken. Most how-to speeches use a sequential design scheme. For instance, if you were to give a speech on how to calibrate a piece of high-tech equipment, or how to make origami cranes, you would probably use a sequential

Speeches that use sequential design follow a step-by-step pattern of development.

design. Sequential designs are most effective when speakers offer a stepwise procedure that makes it easy for audience members to follow.

Chronological. A chronological design explains events or historic developments in the order in which they occurred. Chronological designs often survey the pattern of events that led up to a present-day situation. For example, speakers favoring the privatization of social security sometimes trace the financial history of the program to suggest that it simply will not be there for future generations. Chronological presentations are effective when speakers keep their presentation of events simple, in the order in which they occurred, and related to the message of the speech. Never present a history lesson for its own sake. Use history to illuminate your specific purpose.

Causation. A causation design addresses the causes and/or consequences of a given situation or event. This design proceeds logically from cause to effect or from effect to cause. Causation designs are often used for forecasting future events. For instance, you might give a speech explaining the causes of a budget shortfall on your campus and close by predicting larger class sizes, cuts in student services, and tuition increases. By providing explanations for current events and developments, causation designs satisfy our need for understanding a predictable, if not always controllable, world.

Problem–Solution. The problem–solution design focuses attention on a problem and then provides the audience with potential solutions for resolving it. A popular extension of the problem–solution design, the motivated sequence design follows five steps: (1) calling attention to a situation, (2) demonstrating a need to change it, (3) explaining how that need might be satisfied, (4) visualizing the results of following or not following the speaker's advice, and (5) issuing a call for action. Problem–solution speeches are most effective when they convince audience members that a given problem exists, that the proposed solutions will make a difference, and that these solutions are practical. Effective problem–solution speeches empower listeners by offering ways to change problematic situations.

Refutative. The refutative design is used to speak for or against an issue by repudiating opposing arguments and positions. For example, if you were to give a speech favoring affirmative action on your campus, or opposing a specific type of immigration reform, you might well use a refutative design. This design would include stating opposing views and identifying weaknesses in the reasoning and evidence of opponents. If you suspect that listeners are sympathetic to opposing views, you should concentrate on developing powerful evidence and reasoning that support your position.

Narrative. In contrast to speech designs that follow a linear, logical pattern of development, a narrative design follows a dramatic pattern that proceeds from prologue to plot to epilogue. The **prologue** introduces the story by setting the scene for action. It foreshadows the meaning of the story and introduces the main characters. The **plot** is the body of the narrative. In it, the action of the story unfolds through a

prologue   An opening that establishes the context and setting of a narrative, foreshadows the meaning, and introduces major characters.

plot   The body of a speech that follows narrative design; unfolds in sequence of scenes designed to build suspense.

Figure 9.3

Speech Designs

Categorical	Arranges points in terms of their natural or customary divisions. Useful for organizing large amounts of material. (Chapter 14)
Comparative	Juxtaposes two different ideas so that their similarities and differences are obvious. Useful when a topic is new to listeners or difficult to understand. (Chapter 14)
Spatial	Arranges points as they occur in physical space taking listeners on an orderly tour. (Chapter 14)
Sequential	Arranges points in their order of occurrence. Useful for explaining the steps in a process. (Chapter 14)
Chronological	Arranges points in terms of their development in time. Useful for providing a historical perspective. (Chapter 14)
Causation	Presents the causes and/or effects of a problem. Useful when you want to account for a present situation or forecast future events. (Chapter 14)
Problem-Solution	Discusses a problem and then offers a solution. Useful when your topic involves a situation that needs to be corrected. (Chapter 16)
Refutative	Persuades listeners by repudiating arguments against your position. Useful when you must discredit the opposition. (Chapter 16)
Narrative	Follows the form of a story with a prologue, plot and epilogue. Useful as an indirect form of providing information or persuading listeners. (Chapter 17)

scene or series of scenes that build to a climax. The **epilogue** reflects on the meaning of the story by drawing a lesson from it that audience members can apply to some situation.

While commonly used in introductory and ceremonial speeches, a narrative design can also be incorporated into informative and persuasive presentations to help illustrate and add human interest to the speech.

Whatever design you choose should fit your purpose for speaking, accommodate the main ideas that emerge from your research, and be appropriate for the needs of your audience. For an overview of your design options, see Figure 9.3.

Supporting Your Main Points

Once you have selected and arranged your main points, you should work on subpoints and supporting material. Your subpoints should develop the ideas and information necessary for listeners to accept your main points. For example, assume

epilogue The final part of a narrative that reflects upon its meaning.

you are presenting a speech on the topic "New Developments in the War on Cancer." As you design your speech, you come up with the following main point: "Scientists have transformed medical approaches to researching and treating cancer." To develop this main point, you realize that you must establish two subpoints: "Scientists have largely abandoned the search for a *final cure*" and "Scientists have made tremendous advances in *controlling and living with* cancer."

You strengthen both main points and subpoints by providing supporting materials. As Chapter 8 demonstrated, *facts*, *figures*, and *expert testimony* help support ideas that are disputed, complicated, or new to your audience. *Examples* and *narratives* engage listeners by showing how these ideas apply in specific situations. As powerful as these forms of information may be in isolation, they are more effective when used in combination. An *ideal model of support* includes the most relevant facts and statistics, the most authoritative testimony, and at least one story or example that clarifies your idea and brings it to life. Figure 9.4 provides an outline format for supporting a point.

Consider, for example, how we might support the second subpoint, "Scientists have made tremendous advances in controlling and living with cancer." We would

---

Figure 9.4

Format for Supporting a Point

Statement:_____

_____

Transition into facts or statistics: _____

    1. Factual information or statistics that support statement: _____

_____

_____

Transition into testimony: _____

    2. Testimony that supports statement:_____

_____

_____

Transition into example or narrative: _____

    3. Example or narrative that supports statement:_____

_____

_____

_____

Transition into restatement: _____

Restatement of original assertion:_____

_____

Speaker's Notes 9.1

Determining, Arranging, and Supporting Your Main Points

Follow these steps to determine, organize, and develop your main points.

1. Prepare a research overview to identify repeated ideas.

2. Create main points that fit your purpose and the needs of your audience.

3. Limit your main points to three or fewer for a short speech.

4. Arrange your main ideas using a coherent design.

5. Develop your main ideas with subpoints and supporting material.

want to present factual information concerning latest treatments, drugs, and improved rates of detecting and controlling various forms of cancer that were until recently considered a death sentence. Expert opinions about latest developments in the war on cancer and promising future directions would also help. But our speech would be much more effective and moving if illustrated with the real-life examples and success stories of figures such as Pennsylvania Senator Arlen Specter or seven-time Tour de France winner Lance Armstrong.

Also note how our example illustrates two of the powerful techniques for presenting information that are discussed in Chapter 8. The first is *contrast*, drawn here between past and present research programs, between the dream of a cure and the reality of increasing control over the disease. These contrasts should interest listeners and help them to see your point clearly.

The second technique is *analogy*, especially the figurative analogy between scientific research and war (often seen in such forms as "new weapons," "war on cancer," the researcher as heroic "warrior," etc.). This technique heightens the drama of related narratives and can aid understanding, especially when subjects are complex and abstract. Note how Dr. Leonard Saltz, a colon cancer specialist at Memorial Sloan-Kettering, used another figurative analogy to illustrate the significance of the contrast in research approaches: "I don't think we're going to hit home runs, but if we can get a series of line-drive singles going and put enough singles back to back, we can score runs."[3]

Using Transitions

Once you have determined, arranged, and supported the main points of your speech, you must develop transitions for moving smoothly from point to point. By **transitions**, we mean verbal and nonverbal cues that let your audience know you are finished making one point and are moving on to the next. Effectively planned transitions connect your main points and tie the body of your speech to its introduction and its conclusion. They serve as signposts that help your audience see and follow the overall structure and direction of your speeches.

Some transitions are quite subtle. A brief pause coupled with a change in vocal inflection can cue your audience that you are moving on to the next point or part of your speech. Short, simple phrases such as "For my next point . . ." and "Having said that, I'd like you to consider this . . ." can help your audience see the connection between your ideas. Phrases such as *until now* and *just last week* point out

transitions   Connecting elements used in speeches.

Figure 9.5

Common Transitions

To Indicate	Use
Time Changes	until, now, since, previously, later, earlier, in the past, in the future, meanwhile, five years ago, just last month, tomorrow, following, before, at present, eventually
Additions	moreover, in addition, furthermore, besides
Comparison	compared with, both are, likewise, in comparison, similarly, of equal importance, another type of, like, alike, just as
Contrast	but, yet, however, on the other hand, conversely, still, otherwise, in contrast, unfortunately, despite, rather than, on the contrary
Cause-Effect	therefore, consequently, thus, accordingly, so, as a result, hence, since, because of, due to, for this reason
Numerical Order	first, second, third, in the first place, to begin with, initially, next, eventually, finally
Spatial Relations	to the north, alongside, to the left, above, moving eastward, in front of, in back of, behind, next to, below, nearby, in the distance
Explanation	to illustrate, for example, for instance, case in point, in other words, to simplify, to clarify
Importance	most importantly, above all, keep this in mind, remember, listen carefully, take note of, indeed
The Speech Is Ending	in short, finally, in conclusion, to summarize

time changes. Transitions such as *in addition* show that you are expanding on what you have already said. The use of the word *similarly* indicates that a comparison follows. Phrases such as *on the other hand* cue listeners to a contrast. Cause-and-effect relationships can be suggested with *as a result, consequently,* and similar phrases. Introductory phrases such as *traveling north* can indicate spatial relationships. Phrases or words such as *in short, finally,* or *in conclusion* signal that the speech is coming to an end. Figure 9.5 contains a list of some commonly used transitions.

Preview and summary statements may also be used as effective transitions to connect the major parts of a speech. We discuss these special transitions in the next two sections of this chapter on introducing and concluding your speeches. Sometimes—especially with longer, complicated presentations—an **internal summary** within the body of a speech can help remind listeners of the points you have already covered before moving to your next point. Internal summaries are especially useful in causation and problem–solution speeches, where they signal that you have finished your discussion of the causes or problem and are now going to describe the

internal summary   A transition that reminds listeners of major points already presented in a speech before proceeding to new ideas.

effects or solution. By condensing and repeating your ideas, an internal summary can help listeners remember your message. Consider the following example:

> So now we see what the problem is. We know the cost in human suffering, the terrible political consequences, and the enormous economic burden. The question is, what are we going to do about it? Let me tell you about a plan that experts agree may turn things around.

Preview and summary statements should be brief and to the point so that they highlight only the major ideas in your message.

Speakers sometimes use parallel structure by beginning successive points with similar wording. This pattern itself can signal listeners when you move from one point to another.

Whatever transitional techniques you use, you should plan your transitions carefully. Otherwise, you may ramble awkwardly or over-rely on vocalized pauses such as "uh" and "you know." If you have trouble developing effective transitions, rethink the structure of your message. Outline your thoughts to be sure that they move in a clear direction and in an orderly sequence. We cover outlining in Chapter 10.

Once you have organized the body of your speech—identified and arranged your main points, decided how to develop them with supporting materials, and planned how to connect them with transitions—you should prepare an introduction and conclusion to begin and end your speech effectively. Introductions and conclusions are important because listeners tend to be most affected by what they hear at the beginning and end of a message. The introduction allows you to make a good first impression and to set the stage for how your audience will respond. The conclusion gives you a final opportunity to make a lasting impression.

The introduction of your speech must immediately engage your audience. If you don't get their attention within the first minute of speaking, they may be lost to you forever.

Introducing Your Message

When you first begin to speak, the audience will have three basic questions in mind: *Why should I listen to this speech? Why should I listen to this speaker?* and *What should I understand?* To answer these basic questions, an introduction should capture your audience's attention and involve them with your topic, establish your ethos as a credible speaker, and preview your message to make it easier for the audience to follow.

Capturing Attention

All too often, speakers open their presentations with something like "Good morning. My speech today is on . . . ," and then jump right into their message. Needless to say, this is not a good way to begin a speech because it does not make the audience want to listen. The opening of a speech should arouse attention and involve listeners with the speaker's message. This is especially important when your topic might seem distant from your audience in terms of time, space, and relevance.

There are several ways to attract, build, and hold the interest of your audience as you open your speeches. You might acknowledge the audience, location, or occasion; invoke shared interests and values; solicit audience participation; open with a narrative; use humor; develop suspense; begin with a quotation; or startle your audience.

Acknowledge the Audience, Location, or Occasion. When you speak outside a classroom, it is customary to make some brief opening remarks that acknowledge your audience, the location, or the purpose or meaning of the occasion. People like to hear good things about themselves and their community. Note how Jerry Daniels, president of Boeing Military Aircraft and Missile Systems, opened a speech before the Dayton, Ohio, Chamber of Commerce:

> It's a pleasure to be here at the cradle of aviation—two years and two weeks before the 100th anniversary of the "Miracle at Kitty Hawk." In paying tribute to Orville and Wilbur, historian Darrel Collins noted: "Before the Wright brothers, no one in aviation did anything fundamentally right. Since the Wright brothers, no one has done anything fundamentally wrong."[4]

These introductory remarks can be very brief, but they should also contain a touch of eloquence, as illustrated by the opening words of President John F. Kennedy in a speech given at a White House dinner honoring Nobel Prize winners:

> I think this is the most extraordinary collection of talent, of human knowledge, that has ever been gathered together at the White House, with the possible exception of when Thomas Jefferson dined alone.[5]

With this elegant tribute, Kennedy was able to honor his guests without embarrassing them or going overboard with praise. His reference to the genius of Thomas Jefferson also paid tribute to the past, as did Daniels's reference to the Wright brothers.

Invoking Shared Interests and Values. Invoking shared interests and values is another strategy for capturing audience attention and involving listeners with a topic. Appeals to your listeners' needs for material and financial security can work well in this respect. For example, most young people say they would someday like to marry and have children. Given that assumption about your audience, you might effectively introduce a speech on "new" investment possibilities by citing experts on how expensive it will be to put their future children through college when they reach that age.

Speakers on controversial social or political issues often open by associating the purpose of their speech with moral goals or commitments. Consider the following passage from the introduction to Martin Luther King Jr.'s "I Have a Dream," delivered at the height of the Civil Rights Movement in late summer of 1963:

> Five score years ago, a great American, in whose symbolic shadow we stand today, signed the Emancipation Proclamation. This momentous decree came as a great beacon of light and hope to millions of Negro slaves, who had been seared in the flames of withering injustice. It came as a joyous daybreak to end the long night of their captivity.
>
> But one hundred years later, the Negro is still not free. . . .[6]

Soliciting Audience Participation.   Another opening technique is to solicit the actual participation of audience members. A well-worded series of questions or a simple show of hands can help to promote audience involvement and strengthen audience commitment to your message. Consider the introduction to Beth Tidmore's student speech encouraging audience members to volunteer to work with the Special Olympics:

> Please repeat after me: "Let me win, but if I cannot win, let me be brave in the attempt." [Audience repeats the words.] This is the Special Olympics oath, and this is something that the Special Olympians take every year before they are allowed to compete.
>
> Now, a lot of you have heard what I have to say about Special Olympics. You know the philosophy, you know the history. But what you might not know is what it's like to be a volunteer. . . .

Not all strategies for soliciting audience participation require a direct response. The simple use of inclusive pronouns such as "we" and "our" can help promote identification and involvement with a message. Another technique for promoting the tacit participation of audiences is to use rhetorical questions. **Rhetorical questions** such as "Have you ever thought about what your life would be like if you were a different color?" arouse curiosity and start listeners thinking about the topic. Erin Bourne opened her classroom speech with the following rhetorical question:

> How would you feel if you were a perfect driver—never had a car wreck, never had a speeding ticket—and you got your car insurance bill one day, and it had gone up so high that you could no longer afford to drive? So, you call your insurance company, thinking that there must be some mistake, and they tell you that they had to raise your rates to compensate for all of the not-so-good drivers out there on the road and the claims that they had to pay out for those.
>
> This is analogous to a healthcare problem that is widespread in the United States right now. A few bad doctors are driving malpractice insurance rates up so high in some areas that good doctors are having to either quit practicing medicine or move out of their states.

By posing this rhetorical question and framing the analogy between automobile insurance and medical insurance, Erin gained the attention of her listeners for a topic that otherwise might have seemed distant from them.

Opening with a Narrative.   We humans began our love affair with stories around the campfires of ancient times. Stories help us remember the past and envision the future. They entertain and educate us by framing abstract concerns and challenges in the concrete form of a narrative. They help us "see" a subject in human terms. Stories may be imaginary or based on real-life experiences and historic events. Depending or your purpose for speaking, they may be lighthearted and humorous, or somber and serious. In either case, storytelling is a good way to promote identification and involvement with your message. Introductory narratives should be kept brief. They often rely on vivid language to establish an appropriate mood.

Consider the opening narrative to Ashlie McMillan's introductory speech on scuba diving:

> Imagine you're sitting aboard a dive boat. It's rocking back and forth, you can feel the sun beating down on you. You can feel the wind blowing on you. You

rhetorical questions   Questions that have a self-evident answer, or that provoke curiosity that the speech then proceeds to satisfy.

smell the ocean, the salt water. You can hear the waves crashing up against the boat. You put on your dive pack with your heavy oxygen tank and you walk unsteadily across the deck of the rocking boat. And all of a sudden you plunge into a completely different environment. All around you is vast blueness and infinite space, a world completely different from the one you left above. But all you have to do is turn on your back and look above you and you see the sunlight streaming in through the top of the water. And you can see the world that you left behind.

Ashlie's skillful use of action words—such as *rocking, blowing, crashing*—and her vivid appeal to the senses made this scene come alive for her listeners and placed them in the middle of it.

An opening narrative may also be based on a historical event. Sandra Baltz, a premed major, opened a speech on setting priorities for organ transplants with the following narrative:

On a cold and stormy night in 1841, the ship *William Brown* struck an iceberg in the North Atlantic. Passengers and crew members frantically scrambled into the lifeboats. To make a bad disaster even worse, one of the lifeboats began to sink because it was overcrowded. Fourteen men were thrown overboard that horrible night. After the survivors were rescued, a crew member was tried for the murders of those thrown overboard.

Fortunately, situations like this have been few in history, but today we face a similar problem in the medical establishment: deciding who will live as we allocate scarce medical resources for transplants. Someday, your fate—or the fate of someone you love—could depend on how we resolve this dilemma.

In this example, the story sets a somber mood for the serious message that follows. Stories can also be used to establish a lighter mood through the use of humor.

Appropriate Humor.   Humor can put your audience in a receptive mood for your message. But humor is also one of the most misused techniques for introducing speeches. Because someone once told them that starting with a joke will ensure success, beginning speakers often search through anthologies of "canned humor" to find something that will make people laugh. If you choose to open your speech with humor, keep it fresh and relevant to the situation or your topic. It also should be appropriate for your audience and the occasion, and brief so that it doesn't upstage your message.

Humor can be grossly inappropriate for some topics and occasions. Keep in mind that what you might get away with saying in an informal conversation may be inappropriate, if not offensive, to the same people in a more formal setting. Finally, do not let a humorous introduction trivialize the rest of your speech. We once heard a student open a speech with a rather risqué quotation from Mae West, "Is that a gun in your pocket, or are you happy to see me?" It drew an initial gasp followed by some hearty laughter. Unfortunately, as the speech continued, one student would chuckle over the remembered joke, and then the audience would start laughing all over again even when nothing funny had been said. After the speaker finished, we questioned the audience about their "inappropriate" responses. They said, "We kept remembering that Mae West line. We just couldn't help it." And to this day, none of your authors can remember the topic of the speech, either!

Finally, discover what works for you. Be cautious about using planned humor if you are still coping with communication anxiety. A joke that works can put both a speaker and audience at ease, but one that falls flat can have just the opposite effect. Remember that humor is not a prerequisite for a good speech; there are other ways to come across as likeable and capture audience attention. Play to your strengths.

Develop Suspense.   You can attract and hold your listeners' attention by arousing their curiosity and then making them wait before you satisfy it. The following introduction creates curiosity and anticipation:

> Getting knocked down is no disgrace. Champions are made by getting up just one more time than the opponent! The results are a matter of record about a man who suffered many defeats: Lost his job in 1832, defeated for legislature in 1832, failed in business in 1833, sweetheart died in 1835, had nervous breakdown in 1836, defeated for nomination for Congress in 1843, elected to Congress in 1846, lost renomination in 1848, rejected for land officer in 1849, defeated for Senate in 1854, defeated for nomination for vice president in 1856, defeated for Senate in 1858. In 1860 Abraham Lincoln was elected President of the United States. . . . The greatest failures . . . are those who fail by not doing anything.[7]

The use of humor in an introduction can help set the stage for acceptance of a message.

Reciting the list of failures aroused the audience's curiosity: Who was this loser? Many were surprised when they discovered his identity. This effective introduction set the stage for the speaker's message that perseverance is the key to success.

Begin with a Quotation.   Starting your speech with a striking quotation or paraphrase from a highly respected text or historical figure can both arouse interest and dignify your speech. References to revered political texts such as the Declaration of Independence can command attention. Well-known authors are often gold mines

Speaker's Notes 9.2

Using Humor

Keep the following in mind when considering the use of humor in your speeches.

1. Don't use humor just to be funny. Keep it relevant to your topic.

2. Use humor to put the audience at ease and make them receptive to your ideas.

3. Avoid religious, ethnic, racist, or sexist humor that speaks poorly of you.

4. If you must poke fun at someone, let it be yourself.

5. Don't use humor that might trivialize a serious topic.

6. Avoid planned humor if you are really anxious about speaking.

of eloquence and wisdom. Student speaker David Rasmussen found this nugget among George Orwell's essays: "Every generation imagines itself to be more intelligent than the one that went before it, and wiser than the one that comes after it." David suggested that such arrogance explains the difficulty of passing knowledge from one generation to another. It makes it really hard to talk across time barriers when one generation thinks it is wiser and smarter.

Most effective opening quotations are short and to the point, and they need not come from such elevated sources. Ashlie McMillan used a brief quote from folklore as a lead-in to her informative speech on cystic fibrosis:

> "Woe to the child who when kissed on the forehead tastes salty. He is bewitched and he soon will die." This northern European folk adage is a reference to the genetic disorder cystic fibrosis. Well, we know today that children with cystic fibrosis aren't bewitched. And we have a lot better ways to test for cystic fibrosis than to kiss them on the forehead.

Most books of quotations are indexed by key-words and subjects as well as by authors. Collections of quotations are also available on the Internet. They are an excellent source of statements you might use to introduce your topic. InterConnections.LearnMore 9.1 will guide you to some of these sources.

InterConnections.
LearnMore 9.1

Online Sources of Quotations

Quoteland.com
www.quoteland.com
> *A compilation of quotations from literature, accessible by topic or author.*

Bartleby.com
www.bartleby.com/quotations/
> *A collection of quotations from contemporary and classic sources with a search tool. Provides links to other well-known compendiums of quotations.*

Dictionary of Scientific Quotations
www.naturalscience.com/dsqhome.html
> *A short collection of interesting quotations from scientists.*

Creative Quotations
http://creativequotations. com
> *An excellent source of quotes from over 3,000 famous people. Also contains biographical information on the sources of the quotes. Searchable by key-words and such unique categories as creative women, creative wit, and quotational poetry.*

Good Quotations by Famous People
www.cs.virginia.edu/~robins/quotes.html
> *A compilation of pithy epigrams, such as "Not everything that can be counted counts, and not everything that counts can be counted" (Albert Einstein). Much material that might be useful in introductions and conclusions of speeches. Not categorized by topic or author, but well worth reading through for that special gem you might find! Compiled and maintained by Professor Gabriel Robins, University of Virginia.*

Startle the Audience.   Anything out of the ordinary draws attention to itself and arouses curiosity. This "startle factor" can come in the form of a powerful piece of information or a truly unusual approach to introducing your speech. For instance, opening with a startling statistic such as "One in six American women will be victims of sexual assault—half of them children!" can help to shock and involve your audience. One of our more creative students used the following technique to open his speech:

[Sound of cell phone ringing: speaker takes phone from pocket and speaks into it.]

"Hey!" (pause)

"Nah, that's okay. What's up?"

"Cool!" (short pause, light laugh)

"Yeah! Well, hey, uh—Can I call you back after a while? I'm in my speech class right now—getting ready to give my speech." (pause)

"Okay—just a minute."

[Speaker leaves podium, goes to classmate in front row.]

"Can I borrow your pen? I've got to write down her cell phone number."

[Speaker returns to podium, writes something on speaking outline.]

"Gotta go. Catch you later."

[Speaker pushes phone button, puts cell phone in pocket; long pause, speaker looks around at audience.]

"Sorry 'bout that. Was that rude of me?" (long pause)

Today I want to talk with you about cell phone etiquette, about what annoys other people, and about the polite way to use your phone.

This unusual introduction was so artfully handled that the students thought the student actually had received a call during class. Fortunately, the instructor had been prepped on what to expect, so she didn't stop the speaker before he got started.

The startle technique must always be used with care. You don't want your introduction to arouse more interest than the body of your speech can satisfy. If your

Speaker's Notes 9.3

Capturing Attention

Try the following strategies to gain attention in the introduction of your speech.

1. Acknowledge the audience, location, or occasion.

2. Invoke shared interests and values.

3. Solicit audience involvement and participation.

4. Open with a narrative that relates to your topic.

5. Engage your listeners with appropriate humor.

6. Begin with a striking quotation.

7. Develop a suspenseful introduction.

8. Startle your audience with powerful information or a novel approach.

opening is too sensational, it will upstage the rest of your speech. Similarly, be careful not to go beyond the bounds of propriety. You want to startle your listeners, not offend them.

Establishing Your Credibility

The second major function of an effective introduction is to establish your ethos as a credible speaker. People tend to form first impressions of speakers that color their later perceptions. In Chapter 3, we discussed the importance of developing your ethos in terms of competence, integrity, goodwill, and dynamism. You enter a speaking situation with some initial ethos based on audience members' knowledge of and previous experience with you—what they have learned about you from previous presentations and class discussions.

You can enhance perceptions of your competence by being well organized, using language effectively and correctly, and demonstrating that you know what you are talking about. You will seem more competent if you select a topic you already know something about and have done sufficient research to speak responsibly on it.

Citing relevant training and personal experience at the beginning of your speech can be extremely effective. Michael J. Fox is not a medical scientist, but he has used his own personal struggle with Parkinson's disease to become a credible advocate for stem cell research. Similarly, Lance Armstrong has, through his personal experience and self-education, qualified himself to speak in favor of cancer research. Speakers without such expertise and personal experience can help to establish the competence dimensions of their ethos by citing respected sources of information early in their speeches. The opening of this student speech on consumer culture and advertising follows this guideline:

Calling on personal experience at the beginning of a speech can gain attention and create credibility for the speaker.

> I was amazed to learn in my psychology classes that research does not support a strong link between exposure to persuasive communications and behavior. This discovery led me to do more reading on the relationship between advertising and consumer activity. What I found was even more surprising, especially when you consider that, according to *American Demographics*, advertisers routinely paid over $550,000 for a half minute of air time on *ER*.

To strengthen impressions of integrity, you should try to come across as straightforward, sincere, and genuinely concerned about the consequences of your words. You can accomplish this by demonstrating respect for those who hold different opinions while still maintaining your personal commitment to your topic and position. It should also be clear to your audience that you will not ask more of them than you will ask of yourself. If you demonstrate consideration, understanding, tolerance, and respect, the audience should gain a positive impression of your integrity as a speaker.

You should also present yourself as a likeable and confident speaker, someone who is pleasant and tactful. Likeable speakers treat listeners as friends, inspiring affection in return. They share their feelings and are able to laugh at themselves.

To come across as a confident speaker, you must appear in control of the situation from the outset. Your introduction should reflect your enthusiasm for your message. A smile and eye contact signal listeners that you want to communicate. These qualities build an overall impression of dynamism that should make you more effective.

When you establish favorable ethos in the introduction of your speech, you also lay the foundation for one of the most powerful effects of communication: identification between yourself and listeners. As discussed in Chapter 1, identification helps people overcome the personal and cultural differences that separate them and share thoughts and feelings as though they were one.[8] When you seem likeable, sincere, competent, and dynamic, your listeners want to identify with you, and your effectiveness as a speaker is magnified.

Previewing Your Message

The final function of an introduction is to preview the body of your speech. The **preview** indicates the main points you will cover and offers your listeners an overview of the speech to come. Previews are very useful for speeches on unfamiliar, complicated, or technical subjects. They help listeners follow what you are saying.

Hannah Johnston provided a preview in the introduction to her speech on the perils of fast food:

> I'm sure most of you saw the famous old movie *Soylent Green*. Or, you've heard about the ending, where Charlton Heston finds out what he's really been eating for so long and screams, "Soylent Green is people!"
>
> Well, I'm not saying we need to run around shouting, "McDonald's is feeding us spinal cords," or anything of the sort, but we do need to be aware of a few important things.
>
> First, exactly what ends up in our fast food that shouldn't be there? Second, what conditions in slaughterhouses can lead to mistakes in food preparation? And finally, what are the global health consequences of increased fast-food consumption?

By informing her listeners of her intentions and letting them know how her speech would develop, Hannah helped her audience listen intelligently to her message. Previews are most essential for informative and persuasive speeches. In ceremonial speeches that tell a story rather than develop a topic by logical design, the preview may take the form of a prologue using a **foreshadowing** technique: "I never expected that my life would be forever changed by what would happen that day." When speakers foreshadow their stories, they don't tell their listeners exactly what will happen, but they do alert them that something important will happen. Thus, they prepare them to listen intently to the story.

Selecting and Using Introductory Techniques

A successful introduction can help you as well as your listeners. A smooth presentation of your introduction can ease communication anxiety and carry over into the rest of your speech. Prepare your introduction carefully, and practice it aloud until you are confident and comfortable in your ability to carry it off. Establish eye contact as soon as you rise to speak. Do not read your introduction!

There are no hard and fast rules for determining exactly how you should open a speech. As you review your research notes, look for material that would make an

---

preview   The part of the introduction that identifies the main points to be developed in the body of the speech and presents an overview of the speech to follow.

foreshadowing   Hints to the meaning of the story that will follow.

effective introduction. The following guidelines may help you make a wise selection:

- Consider your audience. Use your introduction to tie your topic to their needs, interests, or well-being.

- Determine the mood you want to establish. Some topics call for a light touch. Others may require you to be more serious.

- Keep it brief. If you are to speak for seven minutes, you can't use a five-minute introduction.

- Do what you do best. Some people are effective storytellers, and others are better at using striking statistics or quotations. Go with your strength!

Developing an Effective Conclusion

Beginning speakers often end their presentations awkwardly. The conclusion of your speech should not be that point at which you just got tired of talking or ran out of time. "That's it, I guess" or "Well, I'm done," and then giving a sigh of relief, suggests that you have not planned your speech carefully. The final words of your speech should stay with listeners, remind them of your message, and when appropriate, move them to action.

Summarizing Your Message

Your conclusion should usually include a summary and final remarks. The more complicated your topic, the more important a summary becomes. A brief **summary** of your main points can serve as a transition between the body of your speech and your final remarks. It signals the audience that you are about to finish.

A summary should not be a simple repetition of the main points of your speech. In his informative speech on the causes of global warming, Josh Logan identified three main sources of the problem: the loss of woodlands around the globe, agricultural and industrial emissions, and personal energy consumption involving especially the use of fossil fuels. Instead of summarizing his speech in a paint-by-numbers manner— "Today I've shown you three causes of the greenhouse effect"—this is what Josh said:

> In conclusion, if you want to understand why global warming has become one of the great crises of our time, you've simply got to step outside into the greenhouse. Listen for the falling trees, watch the industrial smokestacks darkening the sky, and smell that rich bouquet of exhaust fumes that we are constantly pumping into the atmosphere.

By using such colorful language, Josh summarized his main points in a way that listeners would remember.

Concluding Remarks

Although a summary statement can offer listeners a sense of closure, to seal that effect, you need to provide some concluding remarks that stay with your listeners. Many of the techniques that create effective introductions can also be used to develop memorable conclusions.

summary The speaker's reinterpretation of the speech's main ideas at the end of a presentation.

Echo Your Introduction. Sometimes called a "book-end," a conclusion that applies the same technique used in the introduction can help to provide a nice sense of closure. For example, if you begin your speech with a story, you might end with a different story that reinforces the meaning. You might also finish a story that you started in the introduction. Referring back to the introduction can be an effective means of letting listeners know you are bringing your message full circle. For example, the student speaker who told the story of Earl Washington's wrongful conviction for murder in the introduction of her speech echoed this story as she concluded: "The Earl Washingtons out there are counting on you!"

Restate the Relevance to Audience. At the beginning of a speech, you should involve the audience by showing them how your message relates directly to their lives. At the conclusion of your speech, you should remind them of what they personally have at stake. In Josh Logan's informative speech on global warming, the summary statement was followed immediately by remarks that brought the message close to the lives of listeners:

Many persuasive speeches end with a call for action.

> Global warming is a monster of our making. If we don't stop it now, we, our children, and our children's children will have to pay the price: sky-high temperatures, rising seas, violent storms, and a host of dangerous health problems that will make future generations wonder why we sacrificed the quality of their lives. They will ask of us, "How did you let this happen?"

Call for Action. In persuasive speeches, concluding remarks often urge listeners to take the first step to confirm their commitment to action and change. This call for action should make it easy for listeners to comply. Note how Beth Tidmore used the technique to conclude her speech urging her classmates to volunteer for Special Olympics:

> Becoming a volunteer is the best way that you can help. If you can't give a weekend, give a couple of hours. If you can't become a leader, just become a cheerleader. Show up. Be a happy, smiling face. It's the best way to give to charity, because you can see the results right in front of you. You can see the shiny medals, the triumphant finishes, the happy faces, the screaming fans. And you know that you're helping someone else and giving of yourself to them. The benefits are truly rewarding, even if the only thing you get out of it is the satisfaction of knowing you've made a difference.

> Can drives need cans. Blood drives need blood. And, the Special Olympics need volunteers. They need warm hearts and open minds. In Special Olympics, everyone is a winner—especially the volunteers.

At the end of her speech, Beth distributed sign-up forms that helped her listeners make their commitment.

Ask Rhetorical Questions. When used in an introduction, rhetorical questions help arouse attention and curiosity. When used in a conclusion, they give your audience something to think about after you have finished.

Elinor Fraser opened a speech attacking the use of cell phones while driving in the following way: "How many of you were chatting on your cell phones while driving to class this morning?" After a speech that established the danger of such behavior in graphic terms, her final words were:

> "So, now that you know the risk you are running, are you going to use your cell phones again while you're on the way home? If so, let me know so I can drive in a different direction."

End with a Story. Stories are remembered long after facts and figures are forgotten. A concluding narrative can help your audience *experience* the meaning of your message. To end her speech on dangerous off-campus housing conditions, Anna Aley told the following story about her neighbor:

> I got out of my apartment with little more than bad memories. My upstairs neighbor was not so lucky. The main problem with his apartment was that the electrical wiring was done improperly; there were too many outlets for too few circuits, so the fuses were always blowing.
>
> One day last November, Jack was at home when a fuse blew—as usual. And, as usual, he went to the fuse box to flip the switch back on. When he touched the switch, it delivered such a shock that it literally threw this guy the size of a football player backwards and down a flight of stairs. He lay there at the bottom, unable to move, for a full hour before his roommate came home and called an ambulance. Jack was lucky, His back was not broken. But he did rip many of the muscles in his back. Now he has to go to physical therapy, and he is not expected to fully recover.

If time constraints are a consideration, a shorter story may work almost as well. As he concluded his lengthy speech on the New Madrid earthquake zone, Stephen Huff told the following story:

> I now know what I should do if an earthquake hits, but I'm not really sure how I would react. Even the experts don't always react "appropriately." When an earthquake hit the Los Angeles area at about six o'clock one morning, Charles Richter, the seismologist who developed the Richter Scale to measure earthquakes, was in bed at the time. According to his wife, "He jumped up screaming and scared the cat!"

Close with a Quotation. Brief quotations that capture the essence of your message can make for effective conclusions. For example, if one historic quotation opens a speech, another on the same theme or from the same person can provide an elegant sense of closure. Be sure to quote someone the audience respects. In a speech urging students to encourage young children to become volunteers for worthy causes, Rebecca Levinson used the following "classic" quotation:

> Making a difference in the life of a child is a noble thing indeed. When we encourage them to raise money or give of their time to help others, we are helping them prepare to be contributing citizens as adults. In the words of Aristotle, "The habits we form in childhood make no small difference. Rather, they make all the difference."

End with a Metaphor.   A memorable metaphor can end your speech effectively.[9] As we discuss in more detail in Chapter 12, **metaphors** combine things that are apparently unalike so that we see unexpected relationships. In the conclusion of a speech, an effective metaphor may reveal hidden truths about the speaker's subject in a memorable way. Melodie Lancaster, president of Lancaster Resources, used such a metaphor as she concluded a speech to the Houston Council of the American Business Women's Association:

> We recall the story of the three stonemasons who were asked what they were doing. The first said, "I am laying brick." The second replied, "I am making a foundation." And the third said: "I am building a cathedral." Let's you and I set our sights that high. Let's build cathedrals of success today, tomorrow, and the day after tomorrow.[10]

Consider the different meanings this example might evoke in the minds of listeners. First, it suggests that listeners must work hard. Second, it suggests they must work with specific goals in mind. Third, it suggests they must have a vision that gives significance to their work. All these meanings are packed into the metaphor, "building cathedrals of success."

Use Strategic Repetition.   Repetition helps implant ideas in the minds of your listeners. When repetition is combined with parallel construction, in which certain phrases are repeated in close succession for added emphasis, the results can be both elegant and dramatic. Note how Bob Dinneen, president of the Renewable Fuels Association, used this technique to conclude a speech on the use of ethanol to reduce greenhouse gases:

> Who is prepared to stand and take these new steps for change?
> Who is willing to stand up to the skeptics, firm in the conviction that our farmers can produce enough corn to meet the needs of both food and fuel?
> Who is willing to stand and join the effort to reduce greenhouse gases by expanding and improving ethanol technology?
> Who is willing to stand and say, "I'll be the first to commercialize cellulosic ethanal production!"?[11]

Speaker's Notes **9.4**

Techniques for Ending Your Speech

Select from the following techniques to develop an effective conclusion for your speech.

1. Echo your introduction to provide a sense of closure.

2. Point out the relevance of your message to listeners.

3. Issue a call for action to get listeners to confirm their commitment.

4. Ask rhetorical questions that give listeners something to consider after your speech.

5. End with a memorable story that helps listeners experience your message.

6. Close with a quotation that captures the essence of your ideas.

7. End with a metaphor that implants your message in listeners' minds.

8. Use strategic repetition to reinforce your ideas.

metaphor   Brief, concentrated form of comparison that is implied and often surprising. It connects elements of experience that are not usually related in order to create a new perspective.

Selecting and Using Concluding Techniques

Whatever closing technique you choose, be certain that it satisfies your audience that what was promised in the beginning has now been delivered. Plan your summary statement and concluding remarks carefully, just as you did with your introduction. Practice them until you are confident you will end your speech impressively. After your final words, pause a moment to let them sink in, then take your seat.

As with introductions, there are no absolute criteria for deciding what concluding techniques you should use. Here we provide some general guidelines for their selection as we did with selecting introductory techniques:

- Think about what will work best for your audience.

- Consider the message you want your listeners to take with them.

- Use your conclusion to reinforce feelings about your topic.

- Remember time constraints and be brief. Make every word count.

- Play to your strengths as a presenter. Do what you do best.

In Summary

A carefully structured speech helps the audience understand the message and enhances the speaker's ethos.

Good Form. A well-structured speech has good form: It is simple, balanced, and orderly. Simplicity occurs when you limit the number of main points; repeat them for emphasis; and use clear, direct language. A speech has balance when the major parts receive proper emphasis and work together. An orderly speech follows a consistent pattern of development.

Structuring the Body of Your Speech. You should structure the body of your speech first so that you can fashion an introduction and a conclusion that fit your message. To develop the body, determine your main points, decide how to arrange them, and then select effective supporting materials. To identify your main points, prepare a research overview of the information you have collected. This summary can help you spot major themes that can develop into main points.

Arrange your main points so that they fit into a design that is appropriate to the material and that reflects the way people tend to arrange things in their minds. These include categorical, comparative, spatial, sequential, chronological, causation, problem–solution, refutative, and narrative designs.

Supporting materials fill out the speech and buttress ideas. In an ideal arrangement, you should support each point with information, testimony, and an example or story that emphasizes its human aspects.

Using Transitions. Effective transitions point up the relationships among ideas in your speech and tie the speech together. Internal summaries remind listeners of the points you have made in one part of your speech before you move on to another.

Preparing an Effective Introduction. The introduction to a speech should arouse your listeners' interest, establish your credibility, and focus and preview your message. Some useful ways to introduce a speech include acknowledging the audience, location, or occasion; invoking shared interests and values; soliciting audience participation; opening with a narrative; using appropriate humor; beginning with a quotation; developing suspense; and startling the audience. As you build credibility, you also make possible identification between yourself and the audience. When you preview your message, you give your readers the blueprints of the speech that will follow.

Developing an Effective Conclusion. An effective conclusion should review the meaning of your speech in a summary statement, provide a sense of closure, leave the audience with final reflections on the significance of the speech, and if appropriate, motivate listeners to act. Techniques that are useful for conclusions include echoing the introduction, calling for action, reemphasizing relevance to audience, asking rhetorical questions, closing with a quotation, telling a story, ending with a metaphor, and using strategic repetition. Your speech will seem more symmetrical and satisfying if your conclusion ties into your introduction.

Explore and Apply the Ideas in This Chapter

1. Working in small groups, share your research overviews for your next speeches. What major themes emerge, and how might these develop into main points in light of your specific purpose and your listeners' needs? Encourage input from group members to help you select the main points for your speech.

2. Share the organizational plan for your next speech with a classmate so that you become consultants for each other. Help each other come up with alternative patterns for your main points. After the speeches are presented, each consulting team should explain the options it considered and why it chose the particular structure used for each speech.

3. Select a speech from Appendix B and write a thorough critique of its structure. Consider the following questions:

   a. Did this speech satisfy the requirements of "good form"? Did it meet the needs of simplicity, balance, and order?

   b. What design for the main ideas did the speech use?

   c. Did transitions keep the message in focus for listeners?

4. For the same speech critiqued in exercise 3, write an alternative introduction and conclusion, using a different technique. Compare the effectiveness of the new introduction and conclusion with the ones actually used by the speaker. Which work better and why?

5. What type of introductory and concluding techniques might be most effective for speeches based on the following specific purpose statements?

   a. To inform my audience of the steps to follow to get financial assistance.

   b. To persuade my audience that it is better to marry than to live together.

   c. To inform my audience of the signs of child abuse.

   d. To persuade my audience to begin recycling.

10 Outlining Your Speech

Our plans miscarry because they have no aim. When a man does not know what harbor he is making for, no wind is the right wind.

—*Seneca*

As we planned our home on the Tennessee River, we often met with the builders to consider our options. We knew what materials we had to work with, and we had a general sense of what we wanted. But before construction could begin, we would have to make and then remake several important decisions. To help us sort through our choices, our builders developed a series of rough sketches that allowed us to see the relative size, layout, and features of each room in relation to the house as a whole. A later set of blueprints provided the final detailed plans of the home that would rise on the hilltop above the river.

Like a home, a good speech requires careful systematic planning. In Chapter 9, we discussed the process of structuring speeches that are coherent, substantive, and easily remembered. *Outlining is a disciplined process that provides for the final polishing of well-organized speeches.* As with the blueprints to our home, a well-prepared outline helps you see the structure of your presentations as they develop—how your main ideas and supporting materials fit together as they give form to your speech. Outlining assists you in this process in five important ways:

- It objectifies your thinking: It takes ideas out of your head, where they can get all tangled up, and puts them down on paper, where you can see them and work with them.

- It is both a creative and a corrective process. As you think about the relationships among your points, you may come up with new ideas. You can see where you may need more research, whether a point is really relevant, and whether the overall structure is well balanced. You may need to add something here, subtract something there.

- It helps you find and correct problems before they become mistakes.

- It points out where you need transitions.

- It helps you see whether your planned introduction and conclusion actually fit your speech.

In this chapter, we provide sample outline formats that can be adapted for general use. In Chapter 14, we provide abbreviated sample outlines for specific designs that are especially useful in informative speeches: spatial, sequential, chronological, categorical, comparative, and causation. In Chapter 16, we provide abbreviated outlines for the major persuasive speech designs: problem–solution, motivated sequence, and refutative. In Chapter 17, we provide a brief sample outline for the narrative design, which is especially useful in ceremonial speaking.

As you prepare your speech, you may well develop several working outlines, a formal outline, and a key-word outline or note cards to use as a prompt during presentation.

Developing a Working Outline

A working outline helps you to develop a *tentative* plan for your speech. It displays the relationships among your main ideas and allows you to identify potential gaps and trouble spots in your thinking. Assume that you plan to present an informative speech on the greenhouse effect. You have done some research, but you are not completely sure how your speech should develop. Your working outline can help reduce your uncertainty by systematically organizing your thoughts and materials. Outlining forces you to think clearly about the design of your speech. Figure 10.1 provides a format for developing a working outline.

In this early stage of developing your speech, don't worry about the formalities of outlining. Your working outline is simply a tool to help you arrange your thoughts. You should not think of this format as a final structure. Adapt it so that it works for you. You will probably prepare and discard several working outlines before you find the right approach.

A good starting point for your working outline is to write out your specific purpose and thesis statement. As discussed in Chapter 6, your thesis statement should

working outline A tentative plan showing the pattern of a speech's major parts, their relative importance, and the way they fit together.

Figure 10.1

Format for a Working Outline

Topic: _____
Specific purpose: _____
Thesis statement: _____

INTRODUCTION
Attention material: _____
Thesis statement: _____
Preview: _____

(Transition to body of speech)

BODY
First main point: _____
  Subpoint: _____
    Sub-subpoint: _____
    Sub-subpoint: _____
  Subpoint: _____

(Transition to second main point)
Second main point: _____
  Subpoint: _____
  Subpoint: _____
    Sub-subpoint: _____
    Sub-subpoint: _____

(Transition to third main point)
Third main point: _____
  Subpoint: _____
  Subpoint: _____

(Transition to conclusion)

CONCLUSION
Summary statement: _____
Concluding remarks: _____

---

present the central idea of your speech as a short declarative statement. Your specific purpose statement should specify exactly what you want your audience to understand, agree with, do, or appreciate as a result of hearing your speech. Having your specific purpose and thesis statements clearly defined and written out will help you see how well your main points advance them.

Specific purpose: My audience should understand how the greenhouse effect contributes to global warming.

Thesis statement: We must understand the greenhouse effect before we can hope to counter global warming.

Developing Your Main Points

The second step in preparing a working outline is to sketch the body of your speech. Start by selecting and arranging your main points. As you determine these principal

InterConnections.
LearnMore 10.1

Outlining Aids

Basic Outlining

www.lib.jjay.cuny.edu/research/outlining.html

> *A brief online guide to outlining with suggestions for further reading. Developed and maintained by the Lloyd Sealy Library, John Jay College of Criminal Justice.*

Outlining

www.ceap.wcu.edu/Houghton/EDELCompEduc/Themes/Outlining/outlining.html

> *An excellent guide to outlining on your computer. Developed and maintained by Professor Robert S. Houghton, College of Education and Allied Professions, Western Carolina University.*

Organizing Information

www.ipl.org/div/aplus/linksorganizing.htm

> *An online directory of links to Internet sites on outlining and organizing information by cubing, mapping, and more. Developed and maintained by Kathryn L. Schwartz, School of Information, University of Michigan.*

points of focus for your speech, be sure to consider the main themes developed in the research overview described in Chapter 9. Factor in your audience's needs and interests, the specific purpose and thematic statement of your speech, and the amount of time you will have to speak. In our ongoing example of preparing a speech on the greenhouse effect, the *first* working outline contained the following main points:

First main point: Harmful agricultural and industrial emissions accelerate the greenhouse effect.

Second main point: Personal energy consumption magnifies the greenhouse effect.

Third main point: The loss of woodlands adds to the greenhouse effect.

Once you have the main points written out, ask yourself the following questions:

- Will these points make my message clear to my audience?
- Is this the right order in which to develop them?
- Have I left out anything important?

As you consider these questions, you realize that you have left out something important. While you address some prominent *causes* of the greenhouse effect, you do not really explain what it is or why your audience should care. What's more, there is no clear, logical order in your arrangement of main points. However, if you opened by explaining what the greenhouse effect is and why we should care about it, and then proceeded to explain its principle human causes, your speech would more likely involve and inform your listeners. So you revise your first working outline as follows:

First main point: The greenhouse effect is a process by which certain gases in the atmosphere retain the heat of the sun.

Second main point: The loss of woodlands adds to the greenhouse effect.

Third main point: Agricultural and industrial emissions accelerate the greenhouse effect.

Fourth main point: Personal energy consumption magnifies the greenhouse effect.

Developing Subpoints

Once you have determined and arranged your main points, you should develop and support them as discussed in Chapter 9. These more specific statements are the **subpoint** level of your outline. Each main point will be buttressed by two or more subpoints that make it more understandable, believable, or compelling.

To identify the subpoints for each of your main points, imagine a critical listener in front of you. When you state the main point, this listener will want to know:

■ What do you mean?

■ Why should I care?

■ How do I know this is true?

The subpoints for each main point should answer these questions. If the main points are columns built on the foundation of your purpose and thesis statement, the subpoints reinforce these columns so that they will stand up under critical scrutiny. For example, as you develop your working outline, you might list the following subpoints for your first main point:

First main point: The greenhouse effect is a process by which certain gases in the atmosphere retain the heat of the sun.

Subpoints: A. The major greenhouse gases are carbon dioxide and methane.
B. They form a window that holds the heat.
C. This natural process has been unbalanced by human activities.
D. Too many gases are holding in too much heat.
E. Heat waves are breaking temperature records.
F. This situation is causing a climate and health crisis.

You notice that you have listed six subpoints. Recalling the principles of good form learned in Chapter 9, you conclude rightly that you have *too many* subpoints for your speech to be simple, balanced, and orderly.

At this point, you should examine how your subpoints relate to one another. Can you combine any of them? Do you need to break down your subpoints into more specific **sub-subpoints**? For example, you might develop the first main point in this working outline as follows:

First main point: The greenhouse effect is a process by which certain gases in the atmosphere retain the heat of the sun.

Subpoint A: This natural process makes the earth livable.

Subpoint B: Process now unbalanced by human activities.

Sub-subpoints: 1. High concentrations of carbon dioxide and methane in the atmosphere.
2. Heat waves are breaking temperature records.
3. This threatens many living things.

Follow this same procedure as you develop each main point. When you finish, review the working outline of the body of your speech and ask yourself:

■ Will a speech based on this outline satisfy my specific purpose and thesis statement?

■ Will it seem relevant to the interests and concerns of my listeners?

■ Will I be able to accomplish this in the time available?

---

subpoints The major divisions of a speech's main points.

sub-subpoints Divisions of subpoints within a speech.

Speaker's Notes **10.1**

Checklist for a Working Outline

You can trust your working outline if the following statements accurately describe it:

1. My topic, specific purpose, and thesis statement are clearly stated.

2. My introduction contains attention-getting material, establishes my credibility, and focuses and previews my message.

3. My main points represent the most important ideas on my topic.

4. I have an appropriate number of main points for the time allotted.

5. Each subpoint supports its main point with more specific detail.

6. My conclusion contains a summary statement and concluding remarks that reinforce and reflect on the meaning of my speech.

7. I have planned transitions to use between the introduction and body, between each of my main points, and between the body and conclusion of my speech.

Be honest with yourself. It's better to be frustrated now than disappointed after your presentation. In addition, be sure your ideas are arranged in an orderly manner that is easy to follow. Make certain that each subpoint relates directly to the main point above it and that you have enough supporting material to build a strong, responsible structure of ideas. If you are lacking in any of these respects, now is the time to discover and correct the problem.

Completing Your Working Outline

To complete your working outline, prepare an introduction that gains attention, enhances your credibility, and focuses and previews your speech, as we discussed in Chapter 9. Next, develop a conclusion that includes a summary and concluding remarks. Finally, add transitions to tie your speech together. Transitions should connect the introduction to the body, tie each point to the next point as you develop the body, and move the speech from the body to the conclusion.

Now, take a final look at your working outline. (Figure 10.2 is a sample working outline for a speech on global warming.)

Review your outline using the Checklist for a Working Outline in Speaker's Notes 10.1. Go over the outline with someone whose judgment you respect. Another person sometimes can see problems you might miss because you are too close to the material.

As you review your working outline, keep the audience at the center of your thinking. Remember the advice given to beginning journalists: *Never overestimate your audience's information, and never underestimate their intelligence!* Ask yourself the following questions:

- Are my main points arranged so they are easy to follow?

- Do I have sufficient supporting material for each main point?

- Do I have a variety of supporting materials for each main point?

Speech preparation proceeds in fits and starts, periods of frustration followed by moments of inspiration and revision. You may find yourself making and revising several working outlines before you are satisfied.

Figure 10.2

Sample Working Outline

Topic:	The Greenhouse Effect
Specific purpose:	To inform my audience of the significance of the greenhouse effect.
Thesis statement:	We must understand the greenhouse effect before we can hope to counter global warming.

INTRODUCTION

Attention material:	Antarctic icebergs breaking loose: ominous signs of global warming. Nero fiddled while Rome burned: we're fiddling while the Earth burns.
Thesis statement:	We must understand the greenhouse effect before we can hope to counter global warming.
Preview:	We need to be concerned especially about the loss of woodlands, harmful agricultural and industrial emissions, and our own energy consumption.

(**Transition** to body of speech: "Let's begin by understanding the greenhouse effect.")

BODY

First main point:	The greenhouse effect is a process by which certain gases in the atmosphere retain the heat of the sun.
Subpoint A:	This natural process makes the Earth livable.
Subpoint B:	Process now unbalanced by human activities.
Sub-subpoints:	1. High concentrations of carbon dioxide and methane in the atmosphere.
	2. Artificial heat wave is breaking all temperature records.
	3. This threatens Earth's climate and many living things.

(**Transition** to second main point: "Let's examine the causes, one by one.")

Second main point:	The loss of woodlands adds to the greenhouse effect.
Subpoint A:	Loss from cutting.
Subpoint B:	Loss from clearing.
Subpoint C:	Loss from burning.

(**Transition** to third main point: "An even greater cause is harmful agricultural and industrial emissions.")

Third main point:	Agricultural and industrial emissions accelerate the greenhouse effect.
Subpoint A:	Farming an important part of problem.
Sub-subpoints:	1. Frequent tilling and massive CO_2.
	2. Rice farms and methane.
	3. Cattle ranches and more methane.
Subpoint B:	Industrial emissions from burning fossil fuels another big source of problem.

Begin by writing down your topic, specific purpose, and thesis statement so that you have them clearly in mind.

Sketch your introduction, including attention-getting materials. Notice that this first draft omits any direct effort to build credibility. Establishing your credibility on a topic can sometimes be an important strategy early in the speech.

Labeling the body of the speech points out its importance. Be sure to develop the body of the speech first.

Include transitions to remind yourself to tie material together and make it flow smoothly.

The purpose of the working outline is to allow you to organize ideas and see how they fit together. It does not necessarily follow the numbering and lettering of a formal outline.

Figure 10.2

Sample Working Outline (Continued)

(**Transition** to fourth main point: "Finally, let's consider the most important cause
of the runaway greenhouse effect—ourselves.")

Fourth main point: Our personal energy consumption magnifies the
greenhouse effect

    Subpoint A: Both population and prosperity fuel the problem.

      Sub-subpoints: 1. More people = more energy consumption.

          2. Improved living standards add to the problem.

    Subpoint B: Personal energy consumption single largest cause of
greenhouse effect.

      Sub-subpoints: 1. Fossil fuels account for 90% of U.S. personal
energy consumption.

          2. Personal cars tripled since 1950.

(**Transition:** "In conclusion . . .")

CONCLUSION

Summary statement: The greenhouse effect is the key to understanding global
warming. Major causes are loss of woodlands, agricultural
and industrial emissions, and increased personal
consumption.

Concluding remarks: Future generations will ask why we did this to the quality
of their lives.

The working outline serves as a guide and provides a check on the structure of the speech.

Like the introduction, the conclusion is sketched in the working outline. Specific techniques are worked out as outlining proceeds.

Developing a Formal Outline

Once you are satisfied with your working outline, you can prepare your formal outline. Developing a **formal outline** is the final stage of planning and structuring your speeches. It imposes a discipline on your preparation and demonstrates to your instructor that the research and planning phase of your work is completed. The formal outline for a speech typically follows basic conventions of outlining. Figure 10.3 shows a formal speech outline format illustrating these conventions:

1. Identification of speech topic, specific purpose, and thesis statement

2. Separation of speech parts: introduction, body, and conclusion

3. Use of numbering and lettering to display coordination and subordination

4. Wording of main points and subpoints as simple declarative sentences

5. A title

6. A list of major sources consulted

formal outline The final outline in a process leading from the first rough ideas for a speech to the finished product.

Figure 10.3

Format for a Formal Outline

TITLE

Topic: _____
Specific purpose: _____
Thesis statement: _____

INTRODUCTION

Attention material: _____
_____
Thesis statement: _____
_____
Preview: _____
_____

(**Transition** into body of speech)

BODY

I. First main point: _____
   A. Subpoint or supporting material: _____
   B. Subpoint or supporting material: _____
      1. Sub-subpoint or supporting material: _____
      2. Sub-subpoint or supporting material: _____

(**Transition** into next main point)

II. Second main point: _____
   A. Subpoint or supporting material: _____
      1. Sub-subpoint or supporting material: _____
      2. Sub-subpoint or supporting material: _____
   B. Subpoint or supporting material: _____

(**Transition** into next main point)

III. Third main point: _____
   A. Subpoint or supporting material: _____
   B. Subpoint or supporting material: _____
      1. Sub-subpoint or supporting material: _____
      2. Sub-subpoint or supporting material: _____
         a. Sub-sub-subpoint or supporting material: _____
         b. Sub-sub-subpoint or supporting material: _____

(**Transition** into conclusion)

CONCLUSION

Summary statement: _____
_____
Concluding remarks: _____
_____

WORKS CONSULTED

Topic, Specific Purpose, and Thesis Statement

Some student speakers recite their topic, specific purpose, and thesis statement at the beginnings of each speech as though they had been programmed: "My topic is. . . . My specific purpose is. . . . My thesis statement is. . . ." This is not a good way to begin a speech! Nevertheless, you should write these headings out at the top of your outline because they help you focus your message. Just don't read the headings to your audience.

Separation of Speech Parts

As you did in the working outline, separate the introduction, body, and conclusion of the speech so that you give each section the careful attention it requires.

Note from the formal outline format shown in Figure 10.3 that only the body of the speech follows an outlining format. In contrast, the introduction and conclusion should be written out as you plan to speak them. As we suggested in Chapter 3, it is better to write out and commit your introduction and conclusion to memory. Doing so helps you get into and out of your speech gracefully and effectively. Although there may be times when you must adapt and change your introduction in light of the situation (we discussed these moments in relation to context in Chapter 5), as a general rule, a carefully worded beginning works best. Knowing *exactly* what you want to say and how you want to say it gets you off to a good start and helps build your confidence. At the end of your speech, the exact wording of your conclusion can influence whether you make a lasting impression.

Numbering and Lettering Your Outline

Figure 10.3 shows you how to use letters, numbers, and indentation to set up a formal outline that follows the principles of coordination and subordination. The actual number of main points and levels of subpoints may vary, but the basic format remains the same. Roman numerals (I, II, III) identify the main points of your speech. Capital letters (A, B, C) identify the subpoints under each main point. Arabic numbers (1, 2, 3) identify the sub-subpoints under any subpoint.

The principle of **coordination** suggests that all statements at a given level (your *I*'s and *II*'s, *A*'s and *B*'s, and so forth) should be of similar importance and receive similar development. In the sample formal outline shown later in this chapter, the main points include an explanation of the greenhouse effect and its three major causes arranged in ascending order of importance (see Figure 9.1 in the previous chapter). Think how strange it would seem if a fifth main point, "The greenhouse effect will decrease our recreational opportunities," were added to this outline. This statement would not be coordinate in importance with the other

Your outline transfers your ideas for your speech from your head onto a piece of paper.

coordination The requirement that statements equal in importance be placed on the same level in an outline.

main points. Nor would it fit within the pattern of relationships. Adding such a main point would violate the principle of coordination.

The principle of **subordination** requires that material descend in importance from the general and abstract main points to the concrete and specific subpoints and sub-subpoints related to them as shown below:

More important   I. Main point   more general
                     A. Subpoint
                         1. Sub-subpoint
Less important   a. Sub-sub-subpoint   more specific

The more important a statement is, the farther to the left it is positioned. If you rotate an outline clockwise so that it rests on its right margin, the "peaks" will represent the main points, the most important ideas in your speech, with the height of the other points representing their relative significance.

The easiest way to demonstrate the importance of coordination and subordination is to look at an abbreviated sample outline that violates these principles. The following "outlines" a speech of demonstration on how to mat a picture to decorate your dorm room or living quarters:

I.   Decide what color mat to use.
    A. Determine the size of your mat.
    B. Select the proper equipment.

II. You must choose how to back the picture.
    A. How you cut the mat offers options.
    B. Matting the picture requires a decision.

III. Decide between a straight and bevel cut.
    A. Draw lines before you cut.
    B. Plan the project before taking action.

This collection of ideas may look like an outline, but it isn't. It violates the principles of coordination and subordination. The points at each level are not equal in importance, nor are they related to one another. The most basic problems are that the main points—the major steps in the process—have not been clearly identified and their proper order has not been determined. The main points should focus on planning the project, gathering equipment, cutting the mat, and matting the picture. Once you have the main points clearly in place and entered at the Roman numeral level of the outline, you can arrange the subpoints where they fit:

I.   Planning the project should be your first step.
    A. You must decide on the color of your mat.
    B. You must determine its size.
    C. You must select a type of cut.

II. You should gather the equipment you will need.
    A. You will need drawing equipment.
    B. You will need cutting equipment.
    C. You will need matting materials.

III. You can now cut the mat.
    A. Draw the lines for cutting.
    B. Make the cut.

subordination The requirement that material in an outline descend in importance from main points to subpoints to sub-subpoints to sub-sub-subpoints.

IV. Matting the picture is the final step.
   A. Attach the picture to the mat.
   B. Back the picture.

Even the improved version hardly qualifies as a completed outline. The outline would have to proceed to the sub-subpoint level, offering further details, for example, on equipment options, choices among matting materials, and different strategies for cutting. But at least it would be headed *in the direction* of a useful outline, thanks to observing the principles of coordination and subordination.

Wording Your Outline

Each main point and subpoint in your outline should be worded as a simple declarative sentence containing only one idea. It should not be weighted down with qualifying, dependent clauses. For example, the following does not make a good main point sentence:

"Bad eating habits endanger health and lower feelings of self-worth, reducing life span and causing personal anguish." The sentence works better in an outline if it is simplified in the following way:

I.   Bad eating habits are a threat to our well-being.
   A. Bad eating habits endanger health.
      1. They can result in increased heart disease.
      2. They can shorten the life span.
   B. Bad eating habits can damage self-image.
      1. Obese people sometimes dislike themselves.
      2. They can feel that they have nothing to offer others.

Breaking the complex sentence down into outline form helps you to focus what you are going to say. It simplifies and clarifies both the structure and the logic of your speech.

Try to use **parallel construction** when wording the main points of your speech. In parallel construction, *successive sentences or phrases follow the same pattern of wording to emphasize an idea.* If you were developing a speech on the need for reforms in political campaign financing, you might word your main points as follows:

I.   We need reform at the national level.
II.   We need reform at the state level.
III. We need reform at the local level.
IV.   But first, we need to reform ourselves.

If you used these words in the introduction of your speech, the parallel construction would give listeners a guide to the structure of your speech. You could also repeat the parallel pattern as you summarize your speech, further imprinting its message on the minds of your listeners.

Parallel construction has many advantages. Because each sentence has the same basic structure, it can serve as a transition between main ideas. And because any variations tend to stand out sharply, such variation helps to emphasize important points. In this example, the parallel structure helps the speech narrow its focus like a zoom lens as it moves from a national to an individual perspective.

Using parallel construction for your main points can also help you develop internal summaries: "We have looked at reform at the national, state, and local levels, so

parallel construction Wording points in a similar fashion to emphasize their importance and to help the audience remember them.

now we come to the most important part of the problem—ourselves." Since it involves repetition, it makes your message easy to remember. It satisfies the principles of good form, as discussed in Chapter 9.

Supporting Your Main Points

Your formal outline should show how supporting materials fit into your speech. As we noted in Chapter 8, supporting materials strengthen the points you make. For example, a subpoint that states, "Global warming is causing climate changes" might need a factual example and expert testimony to substantiate that claim: "According to statistics from the National Atmospheric and Oceanic Association, the summer of 2006 was the hottest on record." In particular, be sure that each main point receives the type and amount of supporting material it needs to be effective. In Chapter 8, we offered guidelines for deciding what supporting materials you should use if your ideas are controversial, abstract, technical, or distant from the lives of your listeners. In Chapter 9, we described how to work supporting materials into your speech. You should go back and review this material as you prepare your outline.

Title

For speeches given outside the classroom, a title may help attract listeners to a presentation. A good title arouses curiosity. It makes people want to hear the message. You may wish to mention your title in your introduction and then refer to it throughout the speech as a reminder of your thesis statement. However, you don't want to begin your speech by simply stating your title. Rather, find some artful way to weave the title into your introduction in order to focus attention. The following provides a model:

> As I think about the meaning of my speech, I am drawn to my title, "Life in the Greenhouse." How is "Life in the Greenhouse"? I can tell you in one word, "Warm." Warm and getting warmer. Warmer and going global.

You should wait until you have outlined your speech before you select a title. Your title should not promise too much or deceive the audience. Titles that promise everything from eternal peace of mind to the end of taxation often disappoint listeners. Overblown titles also can damage your ethos.

Changing Your Working Outline to a Formal Outline

How can you change your working outline to a formal outline? In the working example provided in Figure 10.2, the third main point appears as follows:

Third main point: Agricultural and industrial emissions accelerate the greenhouse effect.

Subpoint A: Farming an important part of problem.

Sub-subpoints: 1. Frequent tilling and massive CO_2.

2. Rice farms add methane.

3. Cattle ranches add more methane.

Subpoint B: Industrial emissions from burning fossil fuels are another big source of the problem.

To transform this into a formal outline, first, you must use numbering and lettering to indicate coordination and subordination among your points. Second, you should write your points in complete sentences and finish any incomplete structuring, such as we see in subpoint B (it has no sub-subpoints). In the formal outline shown in Figure 10.4, the third main point would take the following form:

III. Farming and industrial practices add more heat to the greenhouse effect (Kluger, "Tipping Point").

  A. Farming is no small part of the problem.
  1. Frequent tilling releases massive CO_2.
  2. Rice farms add methane.
  3. Cattle ranches add still more methane.

  B. Industrial emissions from fossil fuels are a major part of the problem.
  1. Smokestacks strain to produce more energy.
  2. Fleets of trucks crowd the nation's highways.
  3. Flocks of airplanes crisscross the skies.

The final step is to add source citations. Notice that the major source of supporting material (Kluger, "Tipping Point") is indicated in parentheses at the end of the statement of the main point. This brief **source citation** is a cue to the full citation in the list of **works cited** or **works consulted** at the end of the formal outline. Placement of the citation at the end of the main point means that this source supports all claims in the subpoints and sub-subpoints below it. If the citation were placed at the end of a subpoint or sub-subpoint, the citation would apply only to that subpoint or sub-subpoint.

Putting abbreviated source citations in your outline reminds you of the importance of documenting points as you speak. These citations tell your instructor that you have integrated your research into your speech and have met the challenge of acquiring responsible knowledge. Follow these simple guidelines for making brief citations within the outline:

■ List the last name of the author plus the page number when more than one page is cited: (Kluger 34).

■ List the author's last name with an abbreviated title if you are citing more than one work by the same author: (Kluger, "What now?").

■ If the "author" is a group or institution, list the name: (*Science & Space*); if the sponsoring group is not provided, list the first words of the title ("God's Green Soldiers").

Remember: Documenting your sources in your outline does not satisfy the need for oral documentation as you present your speech. Your listeners are not privy to the written citations in your formal outline. Listeners do not really want or need to know every detail offered in these citations. Rather, oral documentation is selective, focusing on the source, source's credentials, the publication, and date as these become more or less relevant to making a point authoritatively and impressively. In other words, you hit the highpoints of your written citations, but you avoid the pedantic repetition of every detail.

Oral documentation in your presentation allows you to give credit where credit is due and to enjoy credit for your own careful research. Citing expert sources as you speak also enhances your ethos and helps forestall any suspicion of plagiarism.

---

source citation References in a speech to sources used.

works cited A form of bibliography in an outline that lists those sources of supporting material actually used in the speech.

works consulted A form of bibliography that lists all sources of research considered in the preparation of the speech.

Figure 10.4

Sample Formal Outline

Title:	Life in the Greenhouse
Topic:	Major Causes of the Greenhouse Effect
Specific Purpose:	To inform listeners of the major causes of the greenhouse effect
Thesis Statement:	Before we can control global warming. we must understand the nature and causes of the greenhouse effect.

INTRODUCTION

Attention Materials: Seas rising along our coastlines. Temperatures setting new records almost every year. Wildfires raging out of control in the West and South. The number and ferocity of hurricanes and tornadoes doubling over the past 30 years. These are the symptoms of global warming, the great environmental disease of our time. But global warming happens because of a phenomenon called "the greenhouse effect."

Thesis Statement: Before we can control global warming, we must understand the nature and causes of the greenhouse effect.

Preview: We need to understand first, the loss of woodlands, second, harmful agricultural and industrial practices, and third, our own personal energy consumption.

(**Transition:** "Let's begin by defining the greenhouse effect.")

BODY

I. The greenhouse effect is a process by which certain gases in the atmosphere retain the heat of the sun (*Science & Space*).
   A. This natural process makes the earth livable.
   B. Process is now unbalanced by human activities.
      1. High concentrations of carbon dioxide have collected in the atmosphere.
      2. Artificial heat wave is breaking all temperature records: 2006 hottest year of the millennium.
   C. This threatens earth's climate and many living things—including us!
(**Transition:** "Let's examine the causes.")

II. Loss of forests adds to the greenhouse effect. (Kluger, "What now?")

   A. Cutting the woods and rain forests for timber is major global problem.
   B. Deliberate burning to create land for farming is even worse.
   C. Wildfires in our country are still another symptom of earth's sickness.
(**Transition:** "Agricultural and industrial emissions are even greater causes of the greenhouse effect.")

III. Farming and industrial practices add more heat to the greenhouse effect (Kluger, "The Tipping Point").

Stating your specific purpose and thesis statement helps you keep them in mind as you outline your speech.

Labeling the introduction shows that it is an important part of the speech.

Examples help gain attention. Citing numerous sources early in the speech enhances credibility.

Previewing the speech helps listeners follow the message.

The use of transitions helps listeners track the progress of the speech.

The first main point defines the greenhouse effect and provides reasons to listen.

Placing the citation at the end of the first point indicates that it is important.

This transition signals a change of focus from explanation to causes.

The causes of the greenhouse effect are arranged in order of increasing importance. Since the loss of woodlands contributes less than the other causes discussed, it receives less attention.

Figure 10.4

Sample Formal Outline (Continued)

The third main point is more developed than the second. The presentation will be more interesting if examples are used.

A. Farming is no small part of the problem.
   1. Frequent tiling releases massive CO_2.
   2. Rice farms add methane.
   3. Cattle ranches add still more methane.
B. Industrial emissions from fossil fuels are a major part of the problem.
   1. Smokestacks strain to produce more energy.
   2. Fleets of trucks crowd the nation's highways.
   3. Flocks of airplanes crisscross the skies.

This transition signals a change of focus.

(**Transition:** "Finally, let's consider the most important cause of the greenhouse effect—ourselves.")

IV. Our personal energy consumption magnifies the greenhouse effect (*Science & Space*).
   A. Both population and prosperity fuel the problem.
      1. More people means more energy consumption.
      2. The quest for better global living standards compounds the problem.
   B. We—the Americans—are the world's greatest energy hogs!
      1. Fossil fuels account for 90% of our personal energy consumption.
      2. Number of personal cars has tripled since 1950.

CONCLUSION

The conclusion creates a startling image as it summarizes the message. It uses rhetorical questions arranged in parallel construction for concluding remarks.

Summary statement: Step outside into the greenhouse. Listen for the falling trees, watch the smokestacks darkening the sky, smell the rich bouquet of fumes.

Concluding remarks: Future generations will ask: Why did we carelessly, willfully, ignorantly allow this to happen to their world? Why did we poison planet Earth?"

WORKS CONSULTED

The references in the works consulted follow the MLA format.

"Global Warming Is Rapidly Raising Sea Levels, Studies Warn," *National Geographic News*, 23 March 2006, http://news.nationalgeographic.com/news/2006/03/0323_060323_global _warming.html.
"God's Green Soldiers," *Newsweek*, 13 Feb, 2006: 49.
"GOP Ex-EPA Chiefs Bash Bush Policies," CNN:com, 18 Jan. 2006, www.cnn.com/2006/POLITICS/01/18/global.warming.ap/index.html, 19 Jan. 2006.
Kluger, Jeffrey, "What now? Our Feverish Planet Badly Needs a Cure," *Time*, 9 Apr. 2007: 51–60.
Kluger, Jeffrey, "The Tipping Point," *Time*, 3 Apr. 2006: 28–42.
"Report: Humans 'Very Likely' Cause Global Warming," *Science & Space*, 2 Feb. 2007, www.cnn.com/2007/TECH/science/02/02/climate.change.report/index.html, 2 Feb 2007.

Speaker's Notes 10.2

Guidelines for Oral Documentation

To develop effective oral documentation, follow these guidelines:

1. Identify the publication in which the material appears.

2. Identify the time frame of the publication.

3. Offer "highlight" credentials for the experts you cite.

4. Select direct quotations that are brief and that will have an impact.

5. Avoid presenting every detail of the written citation.

6. Controversial and time-sensitive material requires fuller oral documentation.

Listing Your References

A list of your major sources of information should appear at the end of your formal outline as "Works Cited" or "Works Consulted." The former lists just those sources you actually cite in your speech; the latter lists all works you consulted during research preparation. Ask your instructor which of these procedures she or he prefers.

The references indicate the range of your research. They are evidence that you have searched for responsible knowledge of your subject. If any of your sources are challenged, the list provides information to validate what you have said. When citing

InterConnections.
LearnMore 10.2
Online Guides to Citation Style

Citing Sources and Avoiding Plagiarism: Documentation Guides
www.lib.duke.edu/libguide/citing.htm

A comprehensive resource that can help you find examples of all types of citations rendered side by side in APA, Chicago, MLA, and Turabian formats. Developed and maintained by Kelley A. Lawton and Laura Cousineau, Duke University Libraries, and Van E. Hillard, The University Writing Program, Duke University.

Columbia Guide to Online Style
www.columbia.edu/cu/cup/cgos2006/basic.html

This well-developed site includes material excerpted from Columbia University Press's hard-copy style guide covering the elements of citation and the preparation of bibliographic material. Contains abundant examples. Developed and maintained by Columbia University Press.

Citing Electronic Documentation: APA, Chicago, and MLA Styles
www.rhetoric.umn.edu/Student/Graduate/%7Emstewart/citations

An up-to-date guide for citing electronic resources using three major style manuals. Contains separate links for the guidelines of each style. Developed and maintained by Professor Mark D. Stewart, Department of Rhetoric, University of Minnesota.

Electronic References
www.apastyle.org/elecref.html

This Web site contains material excerpted from the Publication Manual of the American Psychological Association. You can sign up for automatic e-mail updates and hints issued weekly.

Figure 10.5

MLA and APA Citation Styles

Book: Single Author
MLA   Mann, Thomas. <u>The Oxford Guide to Library Research</u>. New York:
           Oxford UP, 1998.
APA   Mann, T. (1998) <u>The Oxford Guide to Library Research</u>. New York:
           Oxford University Press.

Book: Two or More Authors
MLA   Alexander, Janet E., and Marsha Anne Tate. <u>Web Wisdom: How to
           Evaluate and Create Information Quality on the Web</u>. Mahwah, NJ:
           Lawrence Erlbaum, 1999.
APA   Alexander, J. E., & Tate, M. A. (1999) <u>Web Wisdom: How to
           Evaluate and Create Information Quality on the Web</u>. Mahwah, NJ:
           Lawrence Erlbaum.

Book: Second or Later Edition
MLA   Schlein, Alan M. <u>Find It Online: The Complete Guide to Online Research</u>.
           3rd ed. Tempe, AZ: Facts on Demand Press, 2003.
APA   Schlein, A. M. (2003). <u>Find It Online: The Complete Guide to Online
           Research</u> (3rd ed.). Tempe, AZ: Facts on Demand Press.

Book: Corporate Authors
MLA   American Association of Cereal Chemists. <u>Sweeteners</u>. St. Paul, MN:
           American Association of Cereal Chemists, 1998.
APA   American Association of Cereal Chemists. (1998). <u>Sweeteners</u>. St. Paul,
           MN: American Association of Cereal Chemists.

Signed Article in Reference Work
MLA   Richardson, Brenda L. "Heart Health." <u>Everywoman's Encyclopedia</u>.
           New York: Wellness Press, 2003.
APA   Richardson, B. L. (2003) Heart health. In <u>Everywoman's Encyclopedia</u>
           (pp. 202-206). New York: Wellness Press.

Unsigned Article in Reference Work
MLA   "Musik, Melody." <u>Who's Who in the South, 2003-2004</u>. Mentone, AL:
           Southern Who's Who, 2004.
APA   Musik, Melody (2004). In <u>Who's who in the south, 2003-2004</u> (p. 146).
           Mentone, AL: Southern Who's Who.

Signed Magazine Article
MLA   Stix, Gary. "Ultimate Self-Improvement." <u>Scientific American</u> Sept.
           2003: 44-45.
APA   Stix, G. (2003 September) Ultimate Self-Improvement. <u>Scientific
           American</u>, pp. 44-45.

Unsigned Magazine Article
MLA   "Primary Sources." <u>Atlantic Monthly</u> Nov. 2003: 54-55.
APA   Primary Sources (2003 October). <u>Atlantic Monthly</u>, pp. 54-55.

Figure 10.5

MLA and APA Citation Styles (Continued)

Journal Article

MLA   Barge, J. Kevin. "Hope, Communication, and Community Building."
           Southern Communication Journal 69 (2003): 63-81.

APA   Barge, J. K. (2003). Hope, Communication, and Community Building.
           Southern Communication Journal, 69, 63-81.

Signed Newspaper Article

MLA   Beifuss, John. "Who's Hoping for an Oscar?" Memphis Register 14 Feb.
           2004: E6.

APA   Beifuss, J. (2004, Feb. 14). Who's hoping for an Oscar? Memphis
           Register, p. E6.

Unsigned Newspaper Article

MLA   "It's Gut-check Time," Louisville Chronicle, 23 February 2004: C1.

APA   It's gut-check time. (2004, Feb. 23). Louisville Chronicle, p. C1.

Government Publication

MLA   United States. Environmental Protection Agency. New Motor Vehicles
           and New Motor Vehicle Engines Air Pollution Control: Voluntary
           Standards for Light-Duty Vehicles. Washington, D.C. : Government
           Printing Office, 1998.

APA   U.S. Environmental Protection Agency. (1998). New Motor Vehicles
           and New Motor Vehicle Engines Air Pollution Control: Voluntary
           Standards for Light-Duty Vehicles. Washington, D.C. : Government
           Printing Office.

Personal Interview

MLA   Hogan, Michael. Personal interview. 19 Feb. 2004.

APA   Hogan, M. (2004, February 19). [Personal interview].

Letter or E-Mail Communication

MLA   McGee, Michael Calvin. E-mail to the author. 9 July 2002.

APA   McGee, M. C. (mmcgee@dreammail.net). (2002, July 9). Reply to
           Questions for Book. E-mail to S. Osborn (sso@mailmyth.net).

Speech or Lecture

MLA   Vidulic, Robert. Lecture on dogmatism. Psychology 4231: Social
           Psychology. University of Memphis, 15 March 2004.

APA   Vidulic, R. (2004, March 15). Dogmatism [Lecture]. In Psychology
           4231: Social Psychology. University of Memphis.

World Wide Web Document

MLA   Today: Health. "Can You Spot a Liar?" 29 Jan. 2004.
               <http://www.msnbc.msn.com/id/4072816/> 29 Jan. 2004.

APA   Today: Health. (2004, January 29). Can you spot a liar? [Online].
               Available: http://www.msnbc.msn.com/id/4072816/. [2004, 29
               January].

Speaker's Notes 10.3

Checklist for a Formal Outline

To test the completeness of your formal outline, see if it passes the following tests:

1. My topic and specific purpose are clearly stated.

2. My thesis statement is written as a declarative sentence.

3. My introduction contains material to create attention, establish my credibility, and preview my message.

4. My main points represent the most important ideas on my topic.

5. My main points are similar in importance.

6. My main points are stated as declarative sentences.

7. Each main point is supported by facts, statistics, testimony, examples, or narratives.

8. My subpoints are divisions of the main points they follow and are written as simple sentences.

9. My subpoints are more specific than the main points they follow.

10. My conclusion contains a summary statement and concluding remarks that reflect on the meaning of the speech.

11. I have provided transitions where they are needed to make my speech flow smoothly.

12. I have compiled a list of works cited or consulted in the preparation of my speech.

Internet sources, be sure to provide full citations that include dates accessed so that your instructor can verify your research. The Modern Language Association (MLA) and the American Psychological Association (APA) have published guidelines for constructing such lists. Other protocols include the *Chicago Manual of Style* and the *Turabian Manual for Writers of Term Papers, Theses, and Dissertations*. Ask your instructor which style you should use. For your convenience, Figure 10.5 provides an abridged compilation of the MLA and APA citation formats for the kinds of sources most frequently used in speeches.

After you have completed your formal outline, review it using the Checklist for a Formal Outline in Speaker's Notes 10.3.

Developing a Key-Word Outline

Your formal outline is a blueprint of your speech but not the speech itself. *Do not use your formal outline as you present your speech.* If you do, you will be tempted to read it, which in turn will prevent effective eye contact and authentic interaction with your audience. Instead, you should prepare and speak from a **key-word outline**, usually recorded on index cards, that reduce the main and supporting points of your formal outline to essential words or phrases that will jog your memory and keep you on track during your presentation.

To develop such an outline, simply identify one to three "key" terms in each main point, subpoint, and sub-subpoint and record them on index cards so that they provide an essential overview of the speech. Depending on the length of your speech, you may wish to prepare separate cards for the introduction, the conclusion, and each main point. Include prompts that will remind you to document points. Write out quotations in full on separate cards so that you can quote them with accuracy. You may find it helpful to put your key-word outline on white cards and use colored cards for quotations or material you want to read. Number your cards so you can keep them in order as you speak. Remember that the more cards you carry

key-word outline An abbreviated version of a formal outline that may be used in presenting a speech.

to the lectern, the greater the possibility of confusion. Do not write on both the front and back of note cards.

Keep your note cards as uncluttered as possible so you can refer to them at a glance. *As a general rule, the more your speech is outlined in your head rather than on paper, the better.*

When writing your key-word outline, print in large letters and keep a generous amount of space between points so they stand out clearly. As you practice, add presentation cues to the cards, such as "pause here" or "slow down." Above all, *do not write a mini manuscript of your speech on twenty note cards!* As with trying to speak from a formal "full-sentence" outline, it simply won't work.

Let's return to the third main point of the formal outline on the greenhouse speech to see how it might be turned into a key-word outline format:

Your key-word outline should fit onto a single sheet of paper or a few note cards.

III. Agricultural and industrial **emissions** accelerate the greenhouse effect (Kluger, Turning Point)
   A. **Farming** is an important part of problem.
      1. Frequent **tilling** releases massive CO_2.
      2. **Rice farms** add methane.
      3. **Cattle** ranches add more methane.
   B. **Industrial** emissions from fossil fuels are a major part of problem.
      1. **Smokestacks** strain to produce more energy.
      2. Fleets of **trucks** crowd the nation's highways.
      3. Flocks of **airplanes** crisscross the skies.

In this example, we bold-faced the key-words for the main point, each subpoint, and each sub-subpoint. They then convert into the following key-word format:

III. Cause 2: Emissions (Kluger, TP, Card 3)
   A. Farming
      1. Tilling
      2. Rice farms
      3. Cattle
   B. Industrial
      1. Smokestacks
      2. Trucks
      3. Airplanes (pause for emphasis)

Once you have reduced your speech to a key-word outline, practice using it several times. Speak up, work in your gestures, and force yourself not to look constantly at your cards. Your audience, however, will not notice nor care if you glance occasionally at them, so do not try to hide them. If you are right handed, hold them in your left hand so that you leave the other hand free to gesture. Shuffle your cards from front to back as you move from point to point during your presentation.

When you feel confident that you know your speech, put your notes aside and rest a while before practicing again. If the key-words still jog your memory and keep you on track, you should be ready for your presentation. See Chapter 13 for an extended discussion of rehearsing your speech.

Figure 10.6

Sample Key-Word Outline

Life in the Greenhouse

INTRODUCTION
Global Warming Symptoms

Cause: Greenhouse effect
Need: Understanding

BODY

I. Natural Process (Science card 1)
    A. Makes earth livable
    B. Now unbalanced
        1. high carbon dioxide
        2. ongoing heat wave
    C. Threatens climate—& us!
II. Loss of Forests (Kluger, WN?, card 2)
    A. Timber cutting
    B. Deliberate burns
    C. Wildfires
III. Emissions (Kluger, "TP, card 3)
    A. Farming
        1. tilling
        2. rice farms
        3. cattle
    B. Industrial
        1. smokestacks
        2. trucks
        3. airplanes
III. Personal Use (Science card 4)
    A. Population & prosperity
        1. more people: more use
        2. living standards
    B. We: energy hogs!
        1. fossil fuel

The speaker has added prompts for presentation.

This key-word outline follows the same format used in the formal outline. It contains just enough information to keep the speaker focused on the sequence of points and subpoints. The single words and short phrases prevent the speaker from reading the speech.

In Summary

An outline provides an overview of what you want to say and how you want to say it. It can sharpen and improve the structure of your speech.

Your working outline is a tentative plan of your speech that helps you clarify the relationships among your ideas, shows the relative importance of your points, and depicts how they fit together. By developing working outlines, you can judge the effectiveness of

your research and determine if you need additional material.

The formal outline follows the conventions of coordination and subordination. Coordination requires that statements that are alike in type and importance be at the same level in the outline. Subordination requires that statements descend in importance from main points through subpoints and sub-subpoints. As you descend through these points, they become more specific and concrete.

The main points in a formal outline should be worded as simple declarative sentences containing only one idea. Parallel construction helps listeners remember your message. Source citations provide documentation. Do not forget to provide oral documentation for major evidence and ideas as you present your speech.

A formal outline concludes with a list of works cited or works consulted. The most frequently used formats for such lists are those issued by the Modern Language Association and the American Psychological Association.

A key-word outline reduces the formal outline to a few essential words or phrases that remind you of the content and design of your speech. Notes on the key-word outline can also remind you of presentation strategies. Put quotations on index cards to use during presentation.

Explore and Apply the Ideas in This Chapter

1. Working in small groups, share a working outline for your next speech. Explain your strategy for structure, and show how your outline satisfies the principles of coordination and subordination. Demonstrate that you have adequate supporting materials for each main point in your speech. Revise your outline as appropriate in light of the group discussion that follows.

2. Select one of the speeches from Appendix B and prepare a formal outline of it. Does this outline clarify the structure of the speech? Does it reveal any structural flaws? Can you see any different ways the speaker might have developed the speech? Present your thoughts on these questions in class discussion.

3. Thinking back to the last round of speeches you heard in your class, come up with titles for three of them that could be used in advance advertising to attract an audience.

4. See if you can "unjumble" the following outline of the body of a speech using the principles of coordination and subordination. What title would you suggest for this speech?

Thesis statement: Deer hunting with a camera can be an exciting sport.

    I.   There is a profound quiet, a sense of mystery.
        A. The woods in late fall are enchanting.
            1. The film-hunter becomes part of a beautiful scene.
            2. Dawn is especially lovely.
        B. Time that a big doe walked under my tree stand.
            1. When they appear, deer always surprise you.

            2. How a big buck surprised me after a long stalk.

  II. Hunting from a stand can be a good way to capture a deer on film.
        A. The stalk method on the ground is another way to hunt with a camera.
            1. Learn to recognize deer tracks and droppings.
                a. Learn to recognize deer signs
                b. Learn to recognize rubs and scrapes.
            2. Hunt into the wind and move slowly.
        B. There are two main ways to hunt with a camera.
            1. Stands offer elevation above the deer's line of sight.
            2. Portable stands are also available.
            3. Locating and building your permanent stand.

 III. The right camera can be no more expensive than a rifle.
        A. Selecting the right camera for film-hunting is important.
        B. Certain features, such as a zoom lens, are necessary.

 IV. Display slide of doe.
        A. You can collect "trophies" you can enjoy forever.
        B. Display slide of buck.
        C. You can also use a camcorder.
        D. Not all hunters are killers.
        E. The film-hunter celebrates life, not death.

12 Using Language Effectively

This chapter will help you

- understand the power of language
- apply standards to use language effectively
- learn how to magnify the power of language

Give me the right word and the right accent, and I will move the world.

—Joseph Conrad

A legislator was asked how he felt about whiskey. He replied, "If, when you say whiskey, you mean the Devil's brew, the poison scourge, the bloody monster that defiles innocence, dethrones reason, creates misery and poverty—yes, literally takes the bread from the mouths of little children; if you mean the drink that topples Christian man and woman from the pinnacle of righteous, gracious living into the bottomless pit of degradation, despair, shame and helplessness, then certainly I am against it with all my power.

"But if, when you say whiskey, you mean the oil of conversation, the philosophic wine, the ale that is consumed when good fellows get together, that puts a song in their hearts and the warm glow of contentment in their eyes; if you mean Christmas cheer; if you mean the stimulating drink that puts the spring in an old gentleman's step on a frosty morning; if you mean that drink, the sale of which pours into our treasury untold millions of dollars which are used to provide tender care for our crippled children, our blind, our deaf, our dumb, pitiful, aged and infirm, to build highways, hospitals, and schools, then certainly I am in favor of it.

"That is my stand, and I will not compromise."[1]

The "Whiskey Speech," a legend in southern politics, was originally presented some years ago by N. S. Sweat Jr. during a heated campaign to legalize the sale of liquor-by-the-drink in Mississippi. Because about half of his constituents favored the question and the other half were vehemently opposed, Representative "Soggy" Sweat decided to handle the issue with humor. In the process, he provided an illustration of the magical power of words.

In this chapter, we discuss this power and explain six standards you must satisfy to make language work ethically and effectively in your speeches. We conclude by exploring some special techniques you can use to magnify the power of words.

The Power of the Spoken Word

he ability to use language effectively is one of the most important skills you will ever acquire. There are three important reasons this is so.

1. *Most of us think in words, and the words of our language shape the way we think.* For example, in most parts of the United States, we have just one word for and one conception of snow. However, in the land of the Eskimos, where snow is a constant phenomenon, there are many words to describe it and many ways to think about it.

2. *Language is the basis of all our social interactions.* Our choice of words can determine the success or failure of these interactions.

3. *Words are the essence of our being, of what and how we think about ourselves.* Our language is an integral part of our cultural identity. This becomes especially

important when a language faces the possibility of extinction. D. Y. Begay, a prominent Navajo weaver and art curator, noted, "My father says when you stop speaking the language is when you stop being Navajo."[2]

What Makes the Spoken Word Special

To understand the special powers of the spoken word, we must contrast it with writing.

- **The spoken word is more spontaneous and less formal than the written word.** A journalist might write, "Eight thousand, three hundred twenty-three cases of measles have been reported in Shelby County." But a speaker, communicating the same information, would more likely say, "More than eight thousand cases of measles have been reported in Shelby County!" It's not really important that listeners remember the exact number of cases. What's important is that they see the magnitude of the problem. Rounding off numbers helps listeners focus on the large picture.

- **The spoken word is more colorful and intense than the written word.** These qualities are vital to the effectiveness of communication, as numerous studies of language intensity have demonstrated.[3] Sentence fragments and slang expressions can add to these qualities and are more acceptable in speeches than in essays.

- **Oral language is more interactive, engaging listeners in the feelings and thoughts of the speech as they develop.** Such language depends on audience involvement for its effectiveness. Consider the following excerpt from a speech:

  You want to know what we're going to do? Well, let me tell you what we're not going to do. We're not going to play along! This is a rule that deserves to be broken. Yes, broken! And we're going to do the breaking.

This brief example illustrates the spontaneous, informal, intense, fragmentary, and interactive qualities of oral language. The speaker is keenly aware of her audience. Her words illustrate the conversational character of effective speeches that we discussed in Chapter 1. Moreover, as we discuss in detail in Chapter 13, oral language uses pauses, vocal emphasis, and pitch variations to clarify and reinforce meaning. Such resources are not available in written communication.

- **The spoken word offers special constraints as well as opportunities.** The speaker must remain sensitive to the limitations of live audiences. Communication consultant Jerry Tarver reminds us that listeners cannot "reread" words that are spoken: Oral language must be simpler, and speakers often must repeat themselves to be understood. Speakers may need to amplify ideas with examples to ensure that listeners get the point.[4]

But speakers can arrange the order of words to achieve special impact. Tarver's example is excellent:

  I recently read in a newspaper column a spirited defense of a public figure. The last line of the column was, "For that he should be congratulated, not chastised." Well and good. The reader gobbles up the line in an instant and digests the contrast between congratulations and chastisement. But when

Winston Churchill's radio messages comforted the British people during WWII.

we speak the line we feed it to a listener morsel by morsel. And the last two words prove to be rather bland. We need to hear "For that he should not be chastised, he should be congratulated." More words; but more important, a different order. . . . In the slower pace of speech, individual words stand out more, and thus time accords a special emphasis to the last idea, the climactic idea in the sentence.

As a rule, then, the stronger, more impressive idea should be saved for the end. And it will often be the case that the punch comes from a positive rather than a negative thought.[5]

Tarver's advice to *build up* to your most important point within a sentence repeats a structural principle discussed in Chapter 9—that the main points of a speech often work best when arranged in an order of ascending importance.

Tarver also advises us to take full advantage of the rhythm of oral speech. Spoken language can play on the senses like a drum. The beat of the words can embed them in memory and charge them with emotion. At a low point during World War II, when a German invasion of Great Britain seemed imminent, Prime Minister Winston Churchill spoke on radio to the British people in words that seemed to march in military formation. Read the following language aloud to savor its full oral power:

> We shall not flag nor fail. We shall go on to the end. We shall fight in France and on the seas and oceans; we shall fight with growing confidence and growing strength in the air. We shall defend our island whatever the cost may be; we shall fight on beaches, landing grounds, in fields, in streets and on the hills. We shall never surrender. . . .[6]

■ **When used skillfully, the spoken word has special power to influence listeners.**

1. It can influence how listeners see subjects.
2. It can influence how listeners feel about those subjects.
3. It can influence how listeners identify with one another.
4. It can influence how listeners act.[7]

Understanding this special power—and how it can be abused as well as used—is essential for both speaker and listener.

The Power to Make Listeners See

Speakers and listeners often see subjects in different ways. The artful use of language, however, can close the gap that separates them. Consider, for example, the problem

Speaker's Notes 12.1

Features of the Spoken Word

Consider these features of the spoken word compared to the written word:

1. The spoken word is more spontaneous and less formal.

2. It can be more colorful and intense.

3. It is more interactive and personal.

4. It is simpler, more repetitive, and may need amplification.

5. It arranges the order of language for maximum impact.

6. It takes advantage of rhythm to engage listeners.

7. It can influence how listeners see their world, how they feel about it, how they identify with each other, and how they act.

---

that confronted one of our students, Scott Champlin. Scott wanted to share an experience he had had while serving in the military. One option was to describe the experience matter-of-factly:

> While I was parachuting into Panama as part of Operation "Just Cause," I was wounded by a tracer bullet.

InterConnections.LearnMore:

The Spoken Word

Verbivore: for Lovers of Language

http://verbivore.com

Site devoted to "verbivores," who "feast on the English language." Written and maintained by Richard Lederer, author of Anguished English: An Anthology of Accidental Assaults upon Our Language *(Dell, 1989), it explores the uses and misuses of language; see especially its "Language Links on the Net," a comprehensive guide to classic sites focusing on style, grammar, and the ways of words.*

Power of Words

http://prisonsucks.com/scans/instead_of_prisons/index.shtml

Fascinating study of the power of words in the criminal justice system, especially as language functions as a semantic prison in support of the literal penal system; authors are activists who wish to abolish prisons.

Language as the Tool of Thought

www.bartleby.com/64/

The American Heritage Book of English Usage *offers a practical guide to contemporary English. See especially the sections on style and diction.*

Avoiding Common Errors in English

www.wsu.edu/~brians/errors/index.html

A useful Web site designed to help students keep from sounding unintelligent or ignorant; concentrates mainly on errors of usage in American English; developed and maintained by Professor Paul Brians, Department of English, Washington State University.

But that option seemed less than adequate. How could he use words to convey the *true sense* of that experience? The depiction he developed allowed listeners to share his leap into danger:

> The darkness of two o'clock in the morning was penetrated by streaks of red light marking the paths of tracer rounds as they cut their way through the night. Suddenly, I felt something hit me in the right leg with a force that spun me around like a twisted yo-yo at the end of a string.

Here the use of contrast—between "darkness" and "streaks of red light"—paints a vivid word picture. Action verbs such as *penetrated, cut,* and *spun* enliven the picture. The simile—"like a twisted yo-yo at the end of a string"—brings the picture into sharp focus. Through his artful word choice, Scott was able to share the meaning of his experience.

The power to influence how listeners see things is particularly important when a topic is unfamiliar or unusual. In such cases, your words can become windows that reveal the subject with startling clarity. There can, however, be a negative side to this power of depiction. When listeners don't have a picture of their own to compare with the one revealed by the speaker's words, they are susceptible to deception. Over four hundred years ago, the Renaissance scholar Francis Bacon suggested that the glass in the windows of depiction can be "enchanted": That is, the perspective may be distorted. Words can color or alter things, thus disguising or obscuring reality. The power to make listeners see can also be a power that blinds them.

The Power to Awaken Feelings

Language also can awaken powerful feelings. It can touch listeners and change their attitudes. Nowhere have we seen this power described more eloquently than by twelve-year-old Katherine Stout of Goodlettsville, Tennessee. In her entry in a junior-high school "Letters About Literature" competition sponsored by Humanities Tennessee, Katie wrote: "Words cannot break bones, but they can break hearts."[8] This power of words is used ethically when it *supplements* sound reasoning and credible evidence. It is abused if speakers *substitute* appeals to feelings for evidence or reasoning.

To arouse emotions, language must overcome the barriers of time, distance, and apathy.

Overcoming Time. Listeners live in the present. This makes it difficult for speakers to awaken feelings about events that lie in the remote past or the distant future. To overcome this obstacle, speakers can use language to make the past and future come alive. Stories that recapture feelings from the past are often told at company meetings to re-create the human dimension of the business and to reestablish corporate heritage and culture. In the following story, the speaker reminds listeners of the legend of Federal Express, a pioneer in overnight delivery:

> You know, we take a lot for granted. It's hard to remember that Federal Express was once just a fly-by-night dream, a crazy idea in which a few people had invested—not just their time and their money but their lives and futures. I remember one time early on when things weren't going so well. We were really up against it. Couldn't even make the payroll that week. It looked like we were going to crash. Fred [Smith, founder of the company] was in a deep funk. Never saw him quite like that before or since. "What the hell," he said, and flew off to Las Vegas. The next day he flew back and his face was

shining. "We're going to make it," he said. He had won $27,000 at the black-jack table! And we made it. We met the payroll. And then things began to turn around, and Federal Express grew into the giant it is today.[9]

This story enlivens the past by emphasizing the contrast of emotions—the "deep funk" versus the "shining" face. The use of lively, colloquial dialogue—"What the hell," and "We're going to make it!"—re-creates the excitement and brings those feelings into the present. It would not have been as effective had the speaker simply said, "Fred was depressed, but after he got back from Las Vegas he was confident." Such a bare summary would have distanced the listener and diminished the emotional power of the scene.

Language can also bring the future close to listeners. Because words can cross the barrier of time, both tradition and a vision of tomorrow can guide us through the present.

Overcoming Distance.   The closer anything is to us, the easier it is to develop feelings about it. But what if speakers must discuss faraway people, places, and objects? Words can telescope such subjects and bring them close to hand. Beth Tidmore, our student who won the U.S. Junior Olympics air rifle event at Colorado Springs, demonstrated a special gift for overcoming distance between herself and her listeners.

When she wanted to share her feelings about her shooting experiences, she concentrated on sensory details of touch and smell. "My friends," she said, "don't know what it's like to feel the cold, smooth wood of the cheekpiece against your face. And they don't know the rich smell of Hoppe's No. 9 [oil] when you're cleaning your rifle." Through such sensory descriptions, she was able to communicate with listeners who themselves were far removed from such experiences.

Beth was even more effective when she appealed to her listeners to become involved in Special Olympics events. To move their feelings, Beth used a technique that—when successful—collapses the distance between listeners and subjects. This technique, the vicarious experience narrative, described earlier in Chapter 8, *invites listeners to imagine themselves participating in the action advocated by the speaker.*

> I've had so many great experiences, but these are hard to describe without overworking words like "fulfilling" and "rewarding." So I'm going to let you experience it for yourself. I want everybody to pack your bags—we're going to the Special Olympics summer games in Georgia!

Beth then became a tour guide for her listeners, walking them through the moments that would move them in such dramatic ways. Again, she had effectively bridged the distance between her subject and her audience.

Overcoming Apathy.   We live in an age of communication overkill. Modern audiences are beset with an endless barrage of information, persuasion, and entertainment. As a result, many of us become jaded—we may even develop a *resistance* to communication and turn away from appeals to our feelings and commitment.

Sally Duncan found an especially poignant way to overcome such apathy. Interestingly, it worked because of incompetent language usage. Sally began her informative speech by projecting a picture of her grandmother on the screen behind the lectern. She described her as a cultured, elegant woman who had a masters degree, taught English, and took Sally to art museums and the theater. "Now," she said, "let me read my last letter from Nanny:"

Dear Sally. I am finally around to answer your last. You have to look over me. Ha. I am so sorry to when you called Sunday why didn't you remind me. Steph had us all so upset leaving and not telling no she was going back but we have a good snow ha and Kathy can't drive on ice so I never get a pretty card but they have a thing to see through an envelope. I haven't got any in the bank until I get my homestead check so I'm just sending this. Ha. When you was talking on the phone Cathy had Ben and got my groceries and I had to unlock the door. I forgot to say hold and I don't have Claudette's number so forgive me for being so silly. Ha. Nara said to tell you she isn't doing no good well one is doing pretty good and my eyes. Love, Nanny.

Sally paused for a long moment, and then said, "My Nanny has Alzheimer's." We were riveted as she went on to describe the disease and its effects, and all of us were ready to support any effort to overcome it.

The role of language in arousing feeling is also underscored by the contrast between denotative and connotative forms of meaning. The **denotative meaning** of a word is its dictionary definition or generally agreed-on objective usage. For example, the denotative definition of *alcohol* is "a colorless, volatile, flammable liquid, obtained by the fermentation of sugars or starches, which is widely used as a solvent, drug base, explosive, or intoxicating beverage."[10] How different this definition is from the two connotative definitions offered in this chapter's opening example! **Connotative meaning** invests a subject with the speaker's personal connections and emotions. Thus, the "intoxicating beverage" is no longer just a chemical substance but rather is "the poison scourge" or "the oil of conversation." Connotative language intensifies feelings: Denotative language encourages detachment.

The Power to Bring Listeners Together

In many situations, individual action is not enough. It may take people working together to get things done, and language can bring them together. Words can also bring people together in times of grief. On April 16, 2007, a lone gunman killed 32 innocent victims at Virginia Tech University before turning his gun on himself. At a memorial ceremony the next day, the faculty and student body met to find what comfort they could during those tragic days. The honor of closing the ceremony fell to Nikki Giovanni, an acclaimed poet who was also a University Distinguished Professor. In her remarks, Giovanni combined the power of poetry and prose to express feelings appropriate to the moment:

Poet and professor Nikki Giovanni's eloquent language brought listeners together during a memorial service at Virginia Tech University.

We are Virginia Tech.
We are strong enough to stand tall tearlessly;
We are brave enough to bend to cry
And sad enough to know we must laugh again.
We are Virginia Tech.

denotative meaning The dictionary definition or objective meaning of a word.

connotative meaning The emotional, subjective, personal meaning that certain words can evoke in listeners.

. . . We will continue to invent the future through our blood and tears, through all this sadness . . . . We will prevail![11]

Note the emphasis on "We," the great pronoun of inclusion. Note also how Giovanni combines opposites to create a sense of unity: sadness and laughter, "standing tall tearlessly" and "bending to cry," proposing that a promising future will grow out of the tragic past—that the past and future will come together just as her listeners are brought together by her words.

Although words can unite people, they can also drive them apart. Name calling, exclusionary language, and unsupported accusations can be notorious dividers.

The Power to Encourage Action

Even if your listeners share an identity, they still may not be ready to act. What might stand in their way? For one thing, they may not be convinced of the soundness of your proposal. They may not trust you, or they may not think they can do anything about a problem. Finally, they may not be ready to invest the energy or take the risk that action demands.

Your language must convince listeners that action is necessary, that your ideas are sound, and that success is possible. In her speech urging students to act to improve off-campus housing conditions (see Chapter 16), Anna Aley painted vivid word-pictures of deplorable off-campus housing. She supported these descriptions with both factual examples and her personal experiences. She also reminded listeners that if they acted together, they could bring about change:

> What can one student do to change the practices of numerous Manhattan landlords? Nothing, if that student is alone. But just think of what we could accomplish if we got all 13,600 off-campus students involved in this issue! Think what we could accomplish if we got even a fraction of those students involved!

Anna then proposed specific actions that did not call for great effort or risk. In short, she made commitment as easy as possible. She concluded with an appeal to action:

> Kansas State students have been putting up with substandard living conditions for too long. It's time we finally got together to do something about this problem. Join the Off-Campus Association. Sign my petition. Let's send a message to these slumlords that we're not going to put up with this any more. We don't have to live in slums.

Anna's words expressed both her indignation and the urgency of the problem. Her references to time—"too long" and "it's time"—called for immediate action. Her final appeals to join the association and sign the petition were expressed in short sentences that packed a lot of punch. Her repetition of "slumlords" and "slums" motivated her listeners to transform their indignation into action.

Anna also illustrated another language strategy that is important when you want to move people to action: the ability to depict dramas showing what is at stake and what roles listeners should take.[12] Such scenarios draw clear lines between right and wrong. Be careful, however, not to go overboard with such techniques. Ethical communication requires that you maintain respect for all involved in conflict. As both speaker and listener, be wary of melodramas that offer stark contrasts between good and evil. Such depictions often distort reality.

The Six C's of Language Use

 o harness the power of language in your speeches, your words must meet certain standards: clarity, color, concreteness, correctness, conciseness, and cultural sensitivity. We call these the six C's of oral language.

Clarity

Clarity is the first standard, because if your words are not clear, listeners cannot understand your meaning. This may seem obvious, but it is often ignored! To be clear, you must yourself understand what you want to say. Next, you must find words that convey your ideas as precisely and as simply as possible. Your voice, face, and gestures should help to reinforce the idea as you present it, a process we discuss in Chapter 13. Your listeners must be capable of interpreting your words and nonverbal cues, so they must be able to see and hear you unimpeded by lecterns or by competing noise. The standard of clarity is met when something closely approximating the idea you intend is reproduced in the minds of these listeners.

One factor that impairs clarity is the use of **jargon**, the technical language that is specific to a profession. Such language is often referred to with an *-ese* at the end, as in "speaking computerese." If you use jargon before an audience that doesn't share that technical vocabulary, you will not be understood. For example, "We expect a positive vorticity advective" may be perfectly understandable to a group of meteorologists, but for most audiences, simply saying, "It's going to rain" would be much clearer. Speakers who fall into the jargon trap are so used to using technical language that they forget that others may not grasp it. It does not occur to them that they must translate the jargon into lay language to be understood by general audiences. Adapting technical language so that nonspecialists can understand it can be challenging, but an example in Chapter 8 (page 175), explaining how the OnStar system works in cars, shows how this can be done effectively.

A similar problem is using words that are needlessly overblown and pretentious. A notorious example occurred when signmakers wanted to tell tourists how to leave the Barnum museum. Rather than drawing an arrow with the word Exit above it, they wrote "To the Egress." There's no telling how many visitors left the museum by

jargon Technical language related to a specific field that may be incomprehensible to a general audience.

mistake, thinking that they were going to see that rare creature—a living, breathing "Egress."

Sometimes speakers may deliberately avoid clarity—because the truth may hurt. At moments, these efforts may be rather lighthearted, as when a sports commentator, speaking of the quarterback on a football team, said, "He has ball security issues." The issue he was trying to soften was that the quarterback fumbled a lot. Such efforts to evade and obscure the truth are called **euphemisms**. At other moments, such efforts may seem less innocent. When questioned in 2007 over whether government efforts to find Osama bin Laden should be described as a "failure," a homeland security official responded: "It's a success that hasn't occurred yet."[13]

Even more unethical is the use of words to deliberately befuddle listeners and hide unpleasant truths. One term for such language is **doublespeak**, in which words can point in the direction opposite from the reality they should be describing. (See Figure 12.1.) The *New York Times* charged that the Bush administration developed what they call *ecospeak* (an apparent variation of *doublespeak*) to disguise pro-business and anti-environmental initiatives:

> Mr. Bush . . . may fairly be said to have become the master of the ostensibly ecofriendly sound bite. . . . "Healthy Forests," for instance, describes an initiative aimed mainly at benefiting the timber industry rather than the communities threatened by fire. "Freedom Car" (to be powered by "Freedom Fuel") describes a program to develop a hydrogen-fueled car that, while beguiling in the long term, absolves automakers from making the near-term improvements in fuel economy necessary to reduce oil dependence and the threat of global warming . . . . [In another case] Mr. Bush's purpose was to defend his controversial decision in August to rewrite the Clean Air Act in ways that spared power companies the expense of making investments in pollution controls. . . . His basic argument was that the rules thwarted modernization and economic growth . . . and that his own initiative—dubbed "Clear Skies," in the come-hither nomenclature favored by the White House—would achieve equal results at lower cost.[14]

Figure 12.1

Doublespeak

When they say:	What they often mean is:
Marital discord	Spouse beating
Department of human biodynamics	Department of physical education
Downsizing	Firing
Making a salary adjustment	Cutting your pay
Failed to fulfill wellness potential	Died
Chronologically experienced citizen	Old codger
Initial and pass on	Let's spread the blame
Friendly fire	We killed our own people
Collateral damage	We killed innocent people

euphemism Sometimes humorous use of words to soften or evade the truth of a situation.

doublespeak Using words that point in the direction opposite from the reality they should be describing.

Fearing the reactions of listeners who might actually understand their meaning, such speakers hide behind a cloud of technobabble.

How can you avoid such violations of the clarity standard? One way is through **amplification**, which extends the time listeners have for contemplating an idea and helps them bring it into sharper focus. You amplify an idea by defining it, repeating it, rephrasing it, offering examples of it, and contrasting it with more familiar and concrete subjects. In effect, you tell listeners something and then expand what you have just said. Bill Gates used amplification effectively in his speech on reforming high school education. The following statement from the speech illustrates how definition and contrast especially can clarify an idea:

> America's high schools are obsolete. By obsolete, I don't just mean that our high schools are broken, flawed, and underfunded—though a case could be made for every one of those points.
>
> By obsolete, I mean that our high schools—even when they're working exactly as designed—cannot teach our kids what they need to know today.
>
> Training the workforce of tomorrow with the high schools of today is like trying to teach kids about today's computers on a 50-year-old mainframe. It's the wrong tool for the times.[15]

Color

Color refers to the emotional intensity or vividness of language. Colorful words are memorable because they stand out in our minds. Speakers who use them also are remembered.

In political campaigns, colorful language often gives one candidate an edge over others. During the 1996 presidential primaries, Pat Buchanan became a leading contender, at least partially because of his skill with words. Early in the campaign, another candidate had gained a great deal of attention by proposing tax reform. A third contender, Senator Phil Gramm, criticized this proposal as follows:

> I reject the idea that income derived from labor should be taxed and that income derived from capital should not.[16]

Nice contrast, but about as flat as the tax he was talking about. Now look at how Buchanan expressed the same idea:

> Under Forbes's plan, lounge lizards in Palm Beach would pay a lower tax rate than steelworkers in Youngstown.

Whereas Gramm's words were abstract, Buchanan's were colorful. "Lounge lizards" is striking. So is the use of contrast, setting the "lounge lizards" against steelworkers, Palm Beach against Youngstown. It's sloth and privilege against character and virtue, and we know which side Buchanan is on.

Colorful language paints striking pictures for listeners. Notice how student Leslie Eason made Tiger Woods come alive in her speech of tribute:

> Mothers with daughters of a certain age (mine included) describe him as the son-in-law they'd like to have. Six foot two, a hundred fifty-five pounds, smart—Stanford, remember. Clean cut in his creased khakis, curly hair, gorgeous teeth. Skin the color of what they used to call "suntan" in the Crayola box. And rich. Very rich.

amplification The art of developing ideas by finding ways to restate them in a speech.

He's the very opposite of the gangsta boys in the hood. Boys who wear their pants hanging below their belt as though they were already in the penitentiary. Next to them he's prep school and Pepsodent.

Colorful language is also the key to humor. Note how country humorist "Cotton" Ivy used simple and colorful language to describe his adventures with dieting:

The doctor told me to watch my weight and I got it out there so I can watch it. Anyway, I figured he'd put me on a diet 'cause I can take a shower and my knees not get wet. So Doc said I had to cut back on bread. I said, "Doc, if I don't have bread, what on earth will I use to sop gravy with?" . . . I always thought a balanced diet was a fried pie in each hand.[17]

One very special type of colorful language is **slang**. You've probably been told most of your life not to use slang, that it is a mark of illiteracy and coarseness, that it is vulgar, that it epitomizes "bad" English. But according to general semanticist S. I. Hayakawa, slang can also be "the poetry of everyday life." Or, as the poet Carl Sandburg noted, slang is "language that rolls up its sleeves, spits on its hands, and goes to work."

Slang has its use in speeches: It can add vigor to your message and be a source of identification between you and listeners. But use it with caution. Slang is inappropriate on formal occasions when a high level of decorum is called for. Moreover, you must be certain that your audience will understand your slang. If you have to stop and define your words, they will lose their punch. In such cases, slang will distance you from your listeners, not create identification. You must also be careful about using ethnic slang or other words that your audience might find offensive. Finally, slang should be used sparingly—to emphasize a point or add a dash of humor and color. It should supplement Standard English usage in your speech, not replace it.

Using colorful language makes a speech interesting. It can enhance your ethos by increasing your attractiveness. For these reasons, color is an important standard for the effective use of language.

Concreteness

It is almost impossible to discuss any significant topic without using some abstract words. However, if you use language that is overly abstract, your audience may lose interest. Moreover, because abstract language is more ambiguous than concrete language, a speech full of abstractions invites misunderstanding. Consider this continuum of terms describing a cat.

The Six C's of Effective Language Use

Make certain your language meets these criteria for effective language use.

1. Clarity makes speeches understandable.
2. Color adds punch to your message.
3. Concreteness reduces misunderstandings.
4. Correctness enhances your credibility.
5. Conciseness keeps you from wasting your audience's time.
6. Cultural sensitivity is an ethical imperative.

slang The language of the street.

Mehitabel is a/an

creature	animal	mammal	cat	Persian cat	gray Persian cat

abstract ————————————————————————➤ **concrete**

A similar continuum can be applied to active verbs. If we wanted to describe how a person moves, we could use any of the following terms:

Jennifer

moves	walks	strides

abstract ————————————————————————➤ **concrete**

The more concrete your language, the more pictorial and precise the information you convey. Concrete words are also easier for listeners to remember. Your language should be as concrete as the subject permits.

Correctness

Nothing can damage your credibility more than the misuse of language. Glaring mistakes in grammar can make you seem uneducated and even ignorant. While touting his education plan, one prominent politician told listeners that the most important consideration should be, "Is your children learning?" Other common grammatical errors that make listeners cringe are listed in Figure 12.2.

Mistakes in word selection can be as damaging as mistakes in grammar. Occasionally, beginning speakers, wanting to impress people with the size of their vocabulary, get caught up in the "thesaurus syndrome." They will look up a simple word to find a synonym that sounds more impressive or sophisticated. What they may not realize is that the words shown as synonyms often have slightly different meanings. For example, the words *disorganize* and *derange* are sometimes listed as synonyms. But if you refer to a disorganized person as "deranged," the person's reaction could be interesting.

People often err when using words that sound similar. Such confusions are called **malapropisms**, after Mrs. Malaprop, a character in an eighteenth-century play by Richard Sheridan. She would say, "He is the very *pineapple* of politeness," when she meant *pinnacle*. A prominent baseball player, trying to explain why he had forgotten an appointment for an interview, said, "I must have had *ambrosia*" (which probably caused his *amnesia*, which is what he apparently meant). Archie Bunker, in the classic TV show *All in the Family*, was prone to malapropisms, such as "Don't let your imagination run *rancid*" when he meant *rampant*. William J. Crocker of Armidale College in New South Wales, Australia, collected the following malapropisms from his students:

A speaker can add interest to his talk with an *antidote*. [anecdote]

Disagreements can arise from an unintended *conception*. [Indeed they can! Inference would work better]

The speaker hopes to arouse *apathy* in his audience. [sympathy? empathy?]

Good language can be reinforced by good *gestation*. [gestures]

The speaker can use either an inductive or a *seductive* approach. [deductive][18]

Students, ballplayers, and fictional characters are not the only ones who make such blunders. Elected officials are also not above an occasional malapropism. One former United States senator declared that he would oppose to his last ounce of energy any effort to build a "nuclear waste *suppository*" [repository] in his state. A

malapropisms Language errors that occur when a word is confused with another word that sounds like it.

Figure 12.2

Grammatical Errors

1. Using the wrong tense or verb form:
   Wrong: He *done* us a big favor.
   Right: He *did* us a big favor.

2. Lack of agreement between subject and verb:
   Wrong: *Is* your students giving speeches?
   Right: *Are* your students giving speeches?

3. Using the wrong word
   Wrong: *Caricature* is the most important factor in choosing a mate.
   Right: *Character* is the most important factor in choosing a mate.

4. Lack of agreement between a pronoun and its antecedent:
   Wrong: A hyperactive *person* will work *themselves* to death.
   Right: Hyperactive *people* will work *themselves* to death.
   or
   A hyperactive *woman* will work *herself* to death.

5. Improper type of pronoun used as subject:
   Wrong: *Him* and *me* decided to go to the library.
   Right: *He* and *I* decided to go to the library.

6. Improper type of pronoun used as object:
   Wrong: The speaker's lack of information dismayed my students and *I*.
   Right: The speaker's lack of information dismayed my students and *me*.

7. Double negative:
   Wrong: I *don't never* get good grades on my speeches.
   Right: I *never* get good grades on my speeches.

---

long gone but not forgotten Chicago mayor once commented that he did not believe "in casting *asparagus* [aspersions] on his opponents." And the Speaker of the Texas legislature once acknowledged an award by saying, "I am filled with *humidity*" (perhaps he meant moist hot air as well as humility).

The lesson is clear. To avoid being unintentionally humorous, use a current dictionary to check the meaning of any word you feel uncertain about.

Conciseness

In discussing clarity, we talked about the importance of amplification in speeches. Although it may seem contradictory, you must also be concise, even while you are amplifying your ideas. You must make your points quickly and efficiently.

Simplicity and directness help you be concise. Thomas Jefferson once said, "The most valuable of all talents is that of never using two words when one will do."

Abraham Lincoln was similarly concise as he criticized the verbosity of another speaker: "He can compress the most words into the smallest idea of any man I know." As you work for conciseness, use the active voice rather than the passive in your verbs: "We want action!" is more concise—and more direct, colorful, and clear—than "Action is wanted by us."

You can also achieve conciseness by using **maxims**, those compact sayings that encapsulate beliefs. During the Chinese freedom demonstrations of 1989, a sign carried by students in Tiananmen Square adapted the maxim of Patrick Henry: "Give Me Democracy or Give Me Death." Sadly, the Chinese authorities took them at their word. To reinforce his point that we need to actively (and audibly) confront the problems of racism, sexism, and homophobia, Haven Cockerham, vice president of human resources for Detroit Edison, invented this striking maxim: "Sometimes silence isn't golden—just yellow."[19]

Beyond their conciseness, maxims often evoke cultural memories and invite identification. When the Chinese students adapted the Patrick Henry maxim, they were in effect both declaring that they shared American values and appealing for our assistance in their struggle. When their cause was crushed, many Americans felt the injustice in a personal way, and the resulting tension between the Chinese government and our own lingers to this day.

Maxims have the potential to attract mass-media attention during demonstrations. When printed on signs, they can be picked up as signature statements for movements or campaigns. For example, their brevity and dramatic impact make them well suited to display on television's evening news.

A caution is in order about using maxims. They should not be substituted for a carefully designed and well-supported argument. However, once you have developed a responsible and substantive speech, consider using maxims to reinforce your message.

Cultural Sensitivity

Because words can either lift and unite or wound and hurt your audience, you must exercise **cultural sensitivity** in your choice of language. Looking back into the history of human communication, you will find little about cultural sensitivity. The ancient Greeks, for example, worried only about speaking to other male Athenians who were "free men" and citizens. Today, with the increasing emphasis on empowering diverse cultures, lifestyles, and races and the pursuit of gender equity, cultural sensitivity becomes an important standard for effective language usage.

As we noted in Chapter 5, your classroom audience may represent many different cultures. As listeners, they will be sensitive to clumsy efforts by speakers to identify with folkways that aren't their own. We have already noted how one Republican presidential hopeful offended the Cuban expatriate community. While speaking in Miami, he ended his speech by shouting a political maxim that also, unfortunately, happened to be the favorite sign-off of Fidel Castro's speeches.

Democrats too have had their share of cultural blunders. Once, while speaking in Wisconsin during the 2004 presidential campaign, the democratic candidate, John Kerry, mentioned the much-beloved Green Bay Packers. In the process, however, he referred to Lambeau Field as "Lambert Field." Bad mistake! He had mispronounced the name of "the hallowed grounds on which the Packers play, the frozen tundra of Curly Lambeau Field." Jim VandeHei, writing for the *Washington Post*, pointed up the significance of this boner:

> That's akin to calling the Yankees the Yankers or the Chicago Bulls the Bells.
> This is a place where . . . thousands of fans wear a big chunk of yellow foam

---

maxims Brief and particularly apt sayings.   **cultural sensitivity** The respectful appreciation of diversity within an audience.

Ethics *Alert! 12.1*

The Ethical Use of Powerful Language

To use the power of words in ethical ways, follow these guidelines:

1. Avoid depictions that distort reality: Let your words illuminate the subject, not blind the listener.

2. Use words to support sound reasoning, not substitute for it.

3. Use language to empower both traditions and visions.

4. Use images to renew appreciation of shared values.

5. Use language to strengthen the ties of community, not divide people.

6. Use language to overcome inertia and inspire listeners to action.

7. Be cautious about melodramatic language that reduces complex issues and the people in disputes into good versus evil.

cheese atop their head with the pride of a new parent. "I got some advice for him," [President] Bush told Wisconsinites a few days after the Lambert gaffe. "If someone offers you a cheesehead, don't say you want some wine, just put it on your head and take a seat at *Lambeau* Field."[20]

The seemingly innocent mistake played into the Republican strategy of depicting Kerry as an elitist and a patrician who was uncomfortable with the culture of the people.

A lack of cultural sensitivity almost always has negative consequences. At best, audience members may be mildly offended; at worst, they will be irate enough to reject both you and your message. Cultural sensitivity begins with being attuned to the diversity of your audience and careful about the words you choose. Don't be like the politician who singled out some audience members in wheelchairs for special praise. After lauding their accomplishments, he said, "Now, will you all stand and be recognized?"

Although you must make some generalizations about your audience, avoid getting caught up in stereotypes that suggest that one group is inferior in any way to another. Stay away from racial, ethnic, religious, or gender-based humor, and avoid any expressions that might be interpreted as racist or sexist (see Speaker's Notes 5.1 for guidelines on avoiding racist and sexist language).

Magnifying the Power of Language

There are critical moments in a speech—at the beginning, at the ending, or as arguments reach their conclusions—when you want your words to be most effective. At these moments, you can call on special techniques that magnify the power of language.

The branch of communication study that deals with identifying and understanding these techniques is called *rhetorical style*. Over the centuries, many such techniques have been identified; they seem to be grounded in our nature and to have evolved to meet our need for effective communication. Here we discuss three broad categories of techniques that are especially useful for public speaking: various forms of *figurative language*, techniques that alter the customary *order* of words, and

Cultural sensitivity requires that you be attuned to the diversity of your audience, respectful of the differences between cultural groups, and careful about the words you choose.

techniques that exploit the *sounds* of words for special effects.

Using Figurative Language

Figurative language uses words in surprising and unusual ways. Although many kinds of such language have been identified, we focus on six forms that are especially useful: metaphors, enduring metaphors, similes, personifications, culturetypes, and ideographs.

Metaphors. As we noted in Chapter 8, drawing comparisons is a fundamental way in which our minds work to understand unfamiliar or abstract ideas. A **metaphor** offers a brief, concentrated form of comparison that is implied, unexpected, and sometimes even startling. It connects elements of experience that are not usually related. When you use a metaphor, you pull a rabbit out of a hat. Having read that, your first reaction might be, "Wait a minute, words are not rabbits and language is not a hat!" But when a metaphor works, the listener's next reaction is, "Oooh, I see what you mean!" Good metaphors reveal unexpected similarities in striking ways. They also can add color and concreteness to your message.

Metaphors may be our most useful and versatile stylistic tool. They can be especially helpful in introductions and conclusions. At the beginnings of speeches, metaphors can offer an overall frame of understanding in which a topic can develop. Note how Antoinette M. Bailey, president of the Boeing-McDonnell Foundation, used a wave metaphor to open a speech presented to the International Women in Aviation Conference:

> Suppose we have gone down to the beach on a quiet day. We are standing in the water, admiring the view. Suddenly, a speedboat zooms by at full throttle. Seconds later, we are struck by a powerful wave. This is a bow wave, and it can knock you off your feet if you aren't prepared for it. A very large and fast-moving bow wave is just now beginning to hit the aerospace industry. This morning I want to talk about what we, as an industry, and we, as women, should do to prepare for it.[21]

In a similar vein, concluding metaphors can offer a final frame of understanding that interprets the meaning of a speech for its listeners. When Martin Luther King Jr. spoke to the striking sanitation workers in Memphis the night before he was assassinated, he talked of the "spiritual journey" that his listeners had traveled. He ended his speech by saying that he had climbed the mountain ahead of them—that he had "seen the Promised Land." These metaphors of the journey and the mountain lifted his listeners and allowed them to share his vision, just as he had earlier shared his "dream" with them in his famous "I Have a Dream" oration. More than just communicating in a superficial way, such metaphors may reveal the speaker's soul.

---

figurative language The use of words in certain surprising and unusual ways in order to magnify the power of their meaning.

metaphor Brief, concentrated form of comparison that is implied and often surprising. It connects elements of experience that are not usually related in order to create a new perspective.

Because metaphors can be so powerful, you should select them carefully and use them with restraint. First, *the gravity of the metaphor must match the seriousness of your subject.* Just as you would not typically wear formal attire to a basketball game, you should not use certain metaphors to express certain subjects. If you used Dr. King's mountaintop image to express your overview of the can recycling industry, the effect might be more comic than persuasive.

Second, *mixing metaphors by combining images that don't fit together can confuse listeners and lower their estimation of your competence.* The politician who attacked an opponent saying, "You can't have it both ways in the political process. You can't take the high horse and then claim the low road," mixed his metaphors.

Third, *you also should avoid trite metaphors,* such as "that person [or idea or practice] is so cool" or "I was on an emotional roller coaster." Overuse has turned these metaphors into clichés that no longer affect people. Not only are they ineffective, but using them may again damage your ethos. Tired comparisons suggest a dull mind.

Enduring Metaphors.

One special group of metaphors taps into shared experience that persists across time and that crosses many cultural boundaries. These **enduring metaphors** are especially popular in speeches, perhaps because they invoke experience that has great meaning and that can bring people together. They connect their particular, timebound subjects with timeless themes, such as light and darkness, storms, the sea, disease, and the family. A brief look at three of these metaphors demonstrates their potential power to magnify meaning.[22]

Eloquent language can intensify our feelings about subjects.

Light and Darkness. From the beginning of time, people have made negative associations with darkness. The dark is cold, unfriendly, and dangerous. On the other hand, light brings warmth and safety. It restores control. When speakers use the light–darkness metaphor, they usually equate problems or bad times with darkness and solutions or recovery with light. The speaker's proposal may offer the "dawn," a "candle to light our way," or a "beacon of hope."

Storms and the Sea. The storm metaphor is often used when describing problems. Typically, the storm occurs at sea—a dangerous place under the best of conditions. When political problems are the focus of the speech, the "captain" who "steers the ship of state" can reassure us with his programs or principles—and make them seem very attractive in the process. In his 2001 inaugural address, George W. Bush noted that "through much of the last century, America's faith in freedom and democracy was a rock in a raging sea."[23]

The Family. Family metaphors express the dream of a close, loving relationship among people through such images as "the family of humanity."[24] These metaphors can be especially useful when listeners may feel alienated from each other and from their surroundings. In such situations, family metaphors can be a powerful force to bring listeners together and to effect identification. Wade Steck demonstrated the

enduring metaphors Metaphors of unusual power and popularity that are based on experience that lasts across time and that crosses many cultural boundaries.

potential of such metaphors as he was describing his experiences at the University of Memphis Frosh Camp Program, his introduction to college life:

> As we were riding to camp, my heart was beating really fast. I guess I was kind of nervous—didn't know what I was getting into, wasn't sure I was ready to meet all these new people. But when I got to Frosh Camp, they made me feel at home. First thing they did was to break us into "families" of ten to twelve people who would share the same cabin for those few days. Each "family" had its counselors, carefully selected juniors and seniors who were really called your "mom" and "dad." Sounds corny, I guess, but it did put my mind at ease. . . . The thing I liked most were the Fireside Chats. At night under the stars, watching the logs burn and listening to the crickets chirp, people would just relax and talk about what was in their hearts. I found out those in my family shared my concerns and anxieties. Once we got those out in the open and talked about them, we were ready to go on to college and to start our new lives.

Similarly, the *disease* metaphor pictures our problems as illness and offers solutions in the form of cures.[25] Metaphors of *war and peace* can frame conflict situations and our quest for their resolution.[26] The *building* metaphor, as when we talk about "laying the foundation" for the future, emphasizes our ancient impulse to shape and control the conditions of our lives. And *spatial* metaphors often reflect striving upward and moving forward toward goals.[27]

Perhaps the reason such metaphors are so powerful is that they express the motives we discussed in Chapter 5. Light and darkness, for example, may connect with safety needs (representing our fears as darkness) or esteem and self-actualization needs (representing our successes and growth in terms of light).

Similes.   A **simile** is a variation of metaphor that tips its hand by warning listeners that a comparison is coming. Words such as *like* or *as* function as signals that soften the impact of the expression. The result is to offer a more controlled form of figuration in which the speaker guides the comparison in order to create certain planned effects. One such effect is to help listeners imagine things that are far removed from their experience. Remember Scott Champlin's words, "a force that spun me around *like* a twisted yo-yo at the end of a string"? Most of us, we hope, will never be hit by a tracer bullet while parachuting, but helped by the simile, we can imagine the experience.

A second intended effect is to add interest and concrete focus to experience that may seem dull and remote from listeners' lives. Big business decisions can seem far removed from everyday experience, and not very interesting. But note how John Thorne, a critic of business practices at AT&T, used simile to bring color and interest values to his subject:

> By 1996, AT&T had latched onto a business strategy that *resembled* the actions of a balloonist desperate to clear the Alps. AT&T started heaving things overboard, its smart plays along with the bad plays, in order to stay aloft.[28] [italics added]

Similarly, another critic used simile as a lens to focus her feelings about a presidential proposal to send astronauts on an expedition to Mars: "Spending billions in outer space is *like* buying a new Lexus when the fridge is empty and the roof is leaking."[29]

simile A language tool that clarifies something abstract by comparing it with something concrete; usually introduced by "as" or "like."

A final effect of simile, as all these examples illustrate, is to dramatize a subject so that it appeals to our imagination. As he described reaction to his Oscar-winning film, *An Inconvenient Truth*, Al Gore used simile to place interest in global warming into a dramatic frame: "I've seen times in the past when there was a flurry of concern about global warming, and then, *like* a summer storm, it faded. But this time, it may be different."[30]

Although simile is related to metaphor, it is certainly not the same thing. During the 2004 Democratic primary campaign for the presidency, Howard Dean complained about certain below-the-belt tactics being used against him. When his opponents responded that he himself was guilty of using dehumanizing metaphors, Dean responded in effect that what he had actually used was a simile. Here is how the exchange went, as recorded in *Newsweek*:

> [Interviewer]: There are some people who would say that it takes a little bit of chutzpah for you to complain since at various times you've called the people inside Washington cockroaches—
> [Dean]: That actually is not true. What I said was that they'll be scurrying around in Washington just like cockroaches. That is not calling members of Congress cockroaches.[31]

Dean, at least, believed that there was a substantial difference between metaphor and simile! As the Dean example indicates, you should be careful about the words you choose. When they work well, however, similes can magnify the effect of comparison.

Personifications. One persistent form of figurative speech, **personification**, treats inanimate subjects, such as ideas or institutions, as though they had human form or feeling. The Chinese students who were demonstrating for freedom in Tiananmen Square also carried a statue they called the "Goddess of Liberty." They were borrowing a personification that has long been used in the Western world: the representation of liberty as a woman.[32] When those students then had to confront tanks, and their oppressors destroyed the symbol of liberty, it was easy for many, living thousands of miles away in another culture, to feel even more angry over their fate. Personification makes it easier to arouse feelings about people and values that might otherwise seem abstract and distant.

Culturetypes. **Culturetypes**, sometimes stated in the form of metaphor, express the values, identity, and goals of a particular group and time.[33] In 1960, John F. Kennedy dramatized his presidential campaign by inviting Americans to explore with him "new frontiers" of challenge and discovery. That metaphor worked well in American culture, but it probably would not have made much sense in other countries. For Americans, the frontier is a unique symbol that offers the promise of freedom and opportunity.

Some words that have culturetypal quality include what rhetorical critic Richard Weaver once described as "god and devil terms."[34] He suggested that *progress* has been a primary "god term" of American culture. People often seem willing to follow that word as though it were some kind of divine summons. Tell us to do something in the name of "progress," and many of us will feel obligated to respond. Other terms, such as *science, modern,* and *efficient,* are similarly powerful because they seem rooted in American values. If "science" tells us something, we are apt to listen respectfully. If something is "modern," many of us think it is better, probably

---

personification A figure of speech in which nonhuman or abstract subjects are given human qualities.

culturetypes Terms that express the values and goals of a group's culture.

Ethics *Alert! 12.2*

Questions for Resisting Culturetypes and Ideographs

To become more resistant to the power of certain words, we must cultivate a questioning attitude toward them. The following questions may be helpful:

1. Is the substance of the claim really what it purports to be?

2. Are there hidden motives beneath the surface of words?

3. What values are *not* represented here that ought to be considered?

4. What am I being asked to support or do? Can I defend that position or effort?

because it has benefited from "progress." If something is "efficient," many Americans will more often select it over options that are perhaps more ethical or beautiful. On the other hand, words like *terrorist* and *terrorism* are "devil terms." They can make a person, group, or action seem repulsive and threatening.

Culturetypes can change over time: In recent years, words like *natural*, *communication*, and *environment* have been emerging god terms; *liberalism* and *pollution*, if not devil terms, seem increasingly undesirable.

Ideographs. Communication scholar Michael Calvin McGee identified an especially potent group of culturetypes that he called **ideographs**. These words express a country's basic political values.[35] McGee suggested that words like *freedom*, *liberty*, and *democracy* are important because they are shorthand expressions of political identity. It is inconceivable to us that other nations might not wish to have a "democratic" form of government or that they might not prize "liberty" over every other value. Expressions such as "*freedom* fighters" and "*democracy* in action" have unusual power for us because they utilize ideographs.

As an audience, we can be especially vulnerable to such language, and it can be dangerous. After all, one person's "freedom fighter" can be another person's "terrorist." We must look behind such glittering generalities to inspect the agendas they may hide. You may recall that in Chapter 4 we discussed "trigger words," the idea that we as individuals may react unthinkingly to certain words that trigger emotional response and short-circuit reflection. Ideographs and culturetypes can function as widely shared, cultural trigger words. They are capable of honorable work: They can magnify the appeal of sound arguments, remind us of our heritage, and suggest that we must be true to our values. But the potential for abusing such words in unethical communication is considerable. You must prove that they apply correctly to your topic. As a speaker, use them sparingly, and as a listener, inspect them carefully.

To develop a healthy resistance to such words, we must learn to apply a system of critical questions whenever we encounter them:

1. *Is this really what it claims to be?* For example, does the development of increasingly more powerful weapons of mass destruction really represent "progress"? Are "freedom fighters" actually thugs?

ideographs Compact expressions of a group's basic political faith.

2. *Are those who make these claims legitimate speakers?* For example, are those who advance the "science" of cryonics really "scientists"? Or do they simply exploit our fears of mortality?

3. *Do these claims reflect a proper hierarchy of values?* For example, lopping off the top of a mountain to strip-mine coal may be a highly "efficient" form of mining, but should we be featuring efficiency here? Could protection of the environment be a more important value?

4. *What kinds of actions are these words urging me to endorse or undertake?* For example, should I be asked to support and even die for "democracy" in a nation whose citizens may prefer a different form of government?

Changing the Order of Words

We grow accustomed to words falling into certain patterns in sentences. Strategic changes in the order of words violate these expectations and call attention to the meaning intended. *Antithesis, inversion,* and *parallel construction* all involve changes in the way words are ordered in messages. Their primary functions are to magnify the speaker as a leader and to enhance appeals to action. Let's consider them briefly.

Antithesis. Antithesis arranges different or opposing ideas in the same or adjoining sentences to create a striking contrast. Beth Tidmore used the technique well in her speech on Special Olympics: "With the proper instruction, environment, and encouragement, Special Olympians can learn not only sport skills but life skills." Antithesis also can suggest that the speaker has a clear, decisive grasp of options. It magnifies the speaker as a person of vision, leadership, and action.

President John F. Kennedy often used antithesis in his speeches. Consider these famous words from his Inaugural Address:

> Ask not what your country can do for you—ask what you can do for your country.

You may have learned this quotation in high school and, prompted with the first few words, could probably recite it verbatim today. But Kennedy said essentially the same thing during a campaign speech in September 1960:

> The new frontier is not what I promise I am going to do for you. The new frontier is what I ask you to do for your country.

Same message, different words. The first is memorable; the second is not. The difference is effective antithesis (as well as effective inversion and parallel construction).[36] In its entirety, the passage from the inaugural was as follows:

> And so, my fellow Americans: Ask not what your country can do for you—ask what you can do for your country.
> My fellow citizens of the world: Ask not what America will do for you, but what together we can do for the freedom of man.

Inversion. Inversion reverses the expected order of words in a phrase or sentence to make a statement more memorable and emphatic. Consider how the impact of Kennedy's statement would have been diminished had he used "Do not

---

antithesis A language technique that combines opposing elements in the same sentence or adjoining sentences.

inversion Changing the normal order of words to make statements memorable.

ask" instead of "Ask not." Paul El-Amin concluded his criticism of internment practices after the 9/11 disaster by adapting the same passage from the poem by John Donne: "Ask not for whom the bell tolls. It tolls for me. And it tolls for thee. For all of us who love the Bill of Rights, it tolls." The "ask not" that begins this statement and the final sentence are both inverted from their usual order. The unusual order of the words gains attention and makes the statement impressive. Moreover, the "thee" adds to the impression that this is old, even religious, wisdom. Used in student speeches, inversion works best as a beginning or ending technique, where it can gain attention, add dignity to the effort, and/or frame a memorable conclusion.

At times, inversion goes beyond reversing the expected order of words. In a baccalaureate address presented at Hamilton College, Bill Moyers commented on the many confusions of contemporary life and concluded: "Life is where you get your answers questioned."[37] Here the inversion of the conventional order of thoughts, in which answers usually follow questions rather than the other way around, makes for a witty, striking observation.

Parallel Construction. **Parallel construction** repeats the same pattern of words in a sequence of phrases or sentences for the sake of impact. We discussed the use of parallel construction for framing the main points in a speech in Chapter 10, but parallel construction can occur at any critical moment in a speech. As the Kennedy example illustrates, the repetition of the pattern of words can stamp its message into the mind and make its statement memorable. Perhaps the most famous examples in American public address are Martin Luther King's repeated phrase "I have a dream . . ." in his classic March on Washington speech and Lincoln's "of the people, by the people, and for the people . . ." near the end of the Gettysburg Address. More recently, President George W. Bush also used the technique strikingly. As he announced that military strikes against the Taliban had begun in Afghanistan, the president sounded very much like Winston Churchill as he proclaimed:

> The battle is now joined on many fronts. We will not waver; we will not tire; we will not falter; and we will not fail. Peace and freedom will prevail.[38]

In her tribute to Tiger Woods (see the complete text at the end of Chapter 17), Leslie Eason also used parallel construction in her introduction:

> You're at the Western Open, where Tiger Woods could be Elvis resurrected. People clap when he pulls out the club. They clap when he hits the ball. They clap no matter where that ball lands. They clap if he smiles. They clap because he is.

Exploiting the Sounds of Words

As they are pronounced, words have distinctive sounds. Part of the appeal of parallel construction is that it repeats these sounds. As the Bush example also illustrates, the rhyming of these sounds can add a striking, pleasing effect. At least two other techniques, alliteration and onomatopoeia, also arrange these sounds in distinctive ways. Both techniques magnify the language of feeling.

Alliteration. **Alliteration** repeats the initial sounds in a closely connected pattern of words. One student speaker who criticized the lowering of educational standards paused near the end of her speech to draw the following conclusion: "We don't need the doctrine of dumbing down." Her repetition of the *d* sound was

---

parallel construction Wording points in the same way to emphasize their importance and to help the audience remember them.

alliteration The repetition of initial consonant sounds in closely connected words.

distinctive and helped listeners remember her point. It expressed her strong feeling about practices she condemned.

Onomatopoeia.   **Onomatopoeia** is the tendency of certain words to imitate the sounds of what they represent. For example, suppose you were trying to describe the scene of refugees fleeing from war and starvation. How could you bring that scene into focus for listeners who are far removed from it? One way would be to describe an old woman and her grandson as they *trudge* down a road to nowhere.

Figure 12.3

Magnifying the Power of Language

Using Figurative Language

Technique	Definition	Example
Metaphors	An unexpected figurative comparison	An iron curtain has descended across the continent.
Enduring metaphors	Metaphors that transcend time and cultural boundaries	The development of the Internet marked the dawn of a new way of learning.
Similes	Figurative comparison using *like* or *as*	The jellyfish is like a living lava lamp.
Personifications	Attributing human characteristics to things or events	Liberty raises her flame as a beacon.
Culturetypes	Words that express the values, identity, and goals of a group	This company is devoted to the ideals of modern, efficient, progressive science.
Ideographs	Words that express a country's basic political beliefs	All we ask is liberty and justice.

Manipulating the Order of Words

Technique	Definition	Example
Antithesis	Presenting contrasting ideas in parallel phrases	There is a time to sow and a time to reap.
Inversion	Changing the expected word order	This insult we did not deserve, and this result we will not accept.
Parallel construction	Repetition of words/phrases at beginning or end of sentences	It's a program that ... It's a program that ... It's a program that ...

Exploiting the Sounds of Words

Technique	Definition	Example
Alliteration	Repetition of initial sounds in closely connected words	Beware the nattering nabobs of negativism.
Onomatopoeia	Words that imitate natural sounds	The creek gurgled and babbled down to the river.

---

onomatopoeia The use of words that sound like the subjects they signify.

The very sound of the word "trudge" suggests the weary, discouraged walk of the refugees. Hannah Johnston also used the technique when she described packing-house workers as "literally drenched in a river of blood." By its very sound, *drenched* suggests the unpleasant idea of being soaked with blood as you work. Combined with the "river of blood" metaphor, the technique draws listeners close to what the language describes. Onomatopoeia has this quality of conveying listeners into a scene by allowing them to hear its noises, smell its odors, taste its flavors, or touch its surfaces. The technique awakens sensory experience.

These various ways to magnify the power of language are summarized in Figure 12.3. As you contemplate using them, remember that your words must not seem forced or artificial. For these techniques to work, they must seem to arise naturally and spontaneously in your speaking, and they must seem to fit both you and your subject. You should use them sparingly so that they stand out from the rest of your speech. Used artfully, and in concurrence with the six standards discussed earlier, they can both increase and harness the power of language so that it works productively.

In Summary

Many of us underestimate the power of our words. The language we select can determine whether we succeed or fail as communicators.

The Power of the Spoken Word. Oral language is more spontaneous, less formal, and more interactive than written communication. The spoken word can be more colorful and expansive; it alters the structure of sentences, and it depends more on the rhythm of language as it is voiced.

Words can shape our perceptions. They invite us to see and share the world from the speaker's point of view. They can arouse intense feeling by overcoming the barriers of time, distance, and audience apathy. The spoken word can bring listeners together in a common identity. Finally, words can prompt us to action.

The Six C's of Language Use. As you speak, strive to meet the standards of clarity, color, concreteness, correctness, conciseness, and cultural sensitivity. Clear language is simple and direct: It draws its comparisons from everyday life and avoids jargon.

Color refers to the emotional intensity and vividness of language and is especially vital to the sharing of feeling. The more concrete a word, the more specific the information it conveys. Correctness is vital to ethos because grammatical errors and improper word choices can lower perceptions of your competence. Concise speakers strive for brevity, often using comparisons that reduce complex issues to the essentials. Cultural sensitivity requires that a speaker be aware of the diversity within an audience and respectful of cultural differences.

Magnifying the Power of Language. Certain techniques can magnify the power of words at critical moments in your speeches. Figurative language, techniques that alter the natural order of words, and techniques that exploit the sounds of words are all devices of magnification.

Prominent forms of figurative language are metaphors, enduring metaphors, similes, personifications, culturetypes, and ideographs. Metaphor surprises us with implied, unusual comparisons. Enduring metaphors are rooted in basic human experience and appeal across time and culture. Similes signal and soften the comparison with words such as "like" or "as." Personifications, as in "lady liberty," attribute human form and feeling to inanimate subjects. Culturetypes express the values of a particular people. Ideographs are compact expressions of political faith.

Techniques that alter the natural order of words include antithesis, inversion, and parallel construction. Antithesis arranges opposing ideas in the same or adjoining sentences to create a striking contrast. Inversion reverses the expected order of words in a phrase or sentence to make a statement distinctive. Parallel construction repeats the same pattern of words in a sequence of phrases or sentences for the sake of impact.

Alliteration and onomatopoeia are techniques that exploit the sounds of words. Alliteration repeats initial sounds in a closely connected pattern of words. Onomatopoeia is the tendency of certain words to imitate the sounds of what they represent. Both techniques magnify the language of feeling.

To be effective, all such techniques must seem natural.

Explore and Apply the Ideas in This Chapter

1. What words would you nominate as culturetypes in contemporary society? (Remember, you should be looking for "devil" as well as "god" terms.) Find examples of how these words are used in public communication. Are there any ethical problems with the way these words are used?

2. Analyze how you used the power of language in your last speech. Did you have to overcome any barriers to perception or feeling among your listeners? What techniques did you use? Could you have done better?

3. Look for examples of the use of enduring metaphor in contemporary public communication (speeches, editorials, advertising, visual, and televisual communication). Explain the power of these metaphors by connecting them to motivation as it is explained in Chapter 5.

4. Study the language used in a contemporary political speech. How is the power of language exercised? What special techniques are used to magnify this power? Evaluate the effectiveness of this usage according to the six C's discussed in this chapter: clarity, color, concreteness, correctness, conciseness, and cultural sensitivity.

5. Your instructor will assign different language techniques to members of the class and then present a subject. Your task is to make a statement about this subject, using the technique you have been assigned. Share these statements in class. What does this exercise reveal about the power of the spoken word?

15 Persuasion and Argument

There's a mighty big difference between good, sound reasons and reasons that sound good.

—Burton Hillis

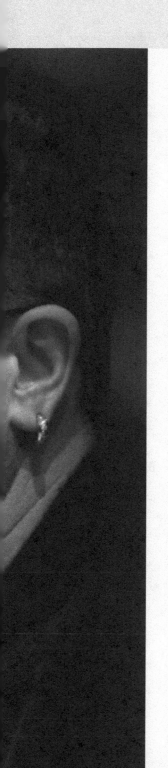

Matthew had a negative reaction to his persuasive speech assignment. "I'm just not a persuader," he fumed, "and I don't want to be one. I make up my own mind on things. I don't like others telling me what to do. I can live without persuasion."

"Not very persuasive," replied his roommate.

Actually, Matthew woke up that morning in a world full of persuasion. As he rubbed the sleep out of his eyes, a DJ on the radio pushed tickets to a rock concert. While he brushed his teeth, his roommate tried to convince him to go to Florida over the break. As he checked his e-mail, he had to wade through spam trying to sell him everything from new cars to a better sex life. Walking to class, someone handed him a flyer protesting the lack of medical services on campus.

For his part, Matthew decided to go to the concert, but not to Florida. He ignored the spam, but could not help but think how a new car might transform his life. On the way back from class, he stopped to argue about the politics of medical care with the person handing out flyers. After he returned to his room, he put on his best clothes for a job interview. He knew that if he got this job, he would constantly have to sell himself and his ideas to others.

Clearly, Matthew needed to rethink the importance of his persuasive speech assignment. In our imperfect world of competing interests, values, and agendas—our world of problems and opportunities—persuasion is unavoidable.

Persuasion works through other people, who can advance or impede our interests and objectives. When we speak, we try to influence how others see things, how they feel, how they believe, and how they act in response to what they learn. We may not always succeed, nor *should* we always succeed: Other views may be more persuasive, depending on the listener, the situation, and the merits of the case. But at least we can give our ideas an opportunity to be heard.

Persuasion, therefore, is the *art of gaining fair and favorable consideration for our points of view.* Persuasion can be ethical or unethical, selfless or selfish, inspiring or degrading. Persuaders may enlighten our minds or prey on our vulnerability. Ethical persuasion, however, is grounded in sound reasoning and is sensitive to the needs and interests of listeners. Ethical persuasion gives us the chance to make the world better.

Realizing that speaking out on public issues is important, many people still ask, "What difference can one person make? My words don't carry much weight." Perhaps not, but words make ripples, and ripples can come together to make waves. Such was the case with Anna Aley, a student at Kansas State University who gave a persuasive speech condemning substandard off-campus student housing. Her classroom speech was later presented in a public forum on campus. The text of her speech, which appears at the end of Chapter 16, was reprinted in the local

persuasion The art of gaining fair and favorable consideration for our point of view.

newspaper, which followed it up with investigative reports and a supportive editorial. Brought to the attention of the mayor and city commission, Anna's speech helped promote reforms in the city's rental housing policies. Her words are still reverberating in Manhattan, Kansas.

Perhaps your classroom speech will not have that kind of impact, but you never know who or what may be changed by it. In this chapter, we explore the nature of persuasive speaking in contrast with informative speaking. Then we turn to using evidence and reasoning to build powerful arguments that provide the substance of ethical and enduring persuasion.

The Nature of Persuasive Speaking

*P*ersuasive speaking differs from informative speaking in eight basic ways:
First, informative speeches reveal options: Persuasive speeches urge a choice among options. Informative speakers expand our awareness. For example, an informative speaker might say: "There are three different ways we can deal with the budget deficit. Let me explain them." In contrast, a persuasive speaker would evaluate these options and urge support for one of them: "Of the three different ways to deal with the budget deficit, we should choose the following course of action."

Second, informative speakers act as teachers: Persuaders act as advocates. The difference is often one of passion and engagement. Persuasive speakers are more vitally committed to a cause. This does not necessarily mean that persuaders are loud; the most passionate and intense moments of a speech can be very quiet.

Third, informative speeches offer supporting material to illustrate points: Persuasive speeches use supporting material as evidence that justifies advice. An ethical persuader interweaves facts and statistics, testimony, examples, and narratives into a compelling case based on responsible knowledge and sensitivity to the best interests of listeners.

Fourth, the role of the audience changes dramatically from information to persuasion. Informed listeners expand their knowledge, but persuaded listeners become *agents of change.* Their new attitudes, beliefs, and actions will affect themselves and others.

Fifth, persuasive speeches ask for more audience commitment than do informative speeches. Although there is some risk in being exposed to new ideas, more is at stake when listening to a persuasive message. What if a persuasive speaker is mistaken or even dishonest? What if her proposed plan of action is defective? Doing always involves a greater risk than knowing. Your commitment could cost you—and those who may be influenced by your actions—dearly.

Sixth, leadership is even more important in persuasive than in informative speeches. Because persuasive speeches involve risk, listeners weigh the character and competence of speakers closely. Do they really know what they are talking about? Do they have their listeners' interests at heart? As a persuasive speaker, your ethos will be on public display and will be scrutinized carefully.

Seventh, appeals to feelings are more useful in persuasive than in informative speeches. Because of the risk involved, listeners may balk at accepting recommendations, even when those recommendations are supported by good reasons. To overcome such inertia, persuaders must sometimes appeal to feelings,[1] which is why they often use emotional appeals to open their speeches. For example, the informative statement "A 10 percent rise in tuition will reduce the student population by about 5 percent next term" might take the following form in a persuasive speech:

Persuasive speeches can help raise support for worthy causes. Here actor Danny Glover speaks out on behalf of the National Kidney Foundation.

The people pushing for the tuition increase don't think a few hundred dollars more each semester will have that much effect. They think we can handle it.

Let me tell you about my friend Tricia. She's on the Dean's List in chemistry, the pride and hope of her family. Tricia will get a great job when she graduates—if she graduates! But if this increase goes through, Tricia won't be back next term. Her dreams of success will be delayed, if not denied!

Perhaps you're in the same boat as Tricia—paddling like mad against the current. We all need to work together to defeat this tuition increase.

Emotional and graphic language, developed through examples or narratives, can help people see the human dimension of problems and move these listeners to the right action.

Eighth, the ethical obligation for persuasive speeches is even greater than that for informative speeches. As Isocrates said (see Chapter 16's opening quotation), persuasion can be a great blessing to humankind. This great educator of the Golden Age of Greece knew that at their best, persuasive speakers make us confront our obligation to believe and act in socially and morally responsible ways. By describing how they themselves became persuaded, they model how we should deliberate in difficult situations. By making intelligence and morality effective in public affairs, they can help the world evolve in more enlightened ways.

The major differences between informative and persuasive speaking are summarized in Figure 15.1.

Figure 15.1

Informative Versus Persuasive Speaking

Informative Speaking	Persuasive Speaking
1. Reveals options.	1. Urges a choice among options.
2. Speaker acts as teacher.	2. Speaker acts as advocate.
3. Uses supporting material to enlighten listeners.	3. Uses supporting material to justify advice.
4. Audience expands knowledge.	4. Audience becomes agent of change.
5. Asks for little audience commitment.	5. Asks for strong audience commitment.
6. Speaker's credibility is important.	6. Speaker's credibility more important.
7. Fewer appeals to feelings.	7. More appeals to feelings.
8. High ethical obligation.	8. Higher ethical obligation.

Argumentative Persuasion

As he finished his speech, "Cooling the World's Fever," Josh Logan knew that he had been effective. Listeners seemed concerned and attentive as he presented his *evidence*. They nodded in agreement as he developed convincing *proofs* to support his points. At the end of the speech, many listeners seemed ready to accept his *argument* that global warming would require far-reaching changes both at the government level and in the ways people lived.

Some persuasive efforts lift and inspire us, while others seem degrading. What is the critical difference? There is a kind of persuasion—**manipulative persuasion**—that has become part and parcel of life in media America. Such persuasion works by suggestion, colorful images, appealing music, and attractive spokespersons. It reveals itself in thirty-second television commercials that sell us everything from deodorant to political candidates. In his recent book, *The Assault on Reason*, Al Gore argues that contemporary politics especially attracts the manipulator and compromises the quality of persuasive discourse:

> Voters are often viewed mainly as targets for easy manipulation by those seeking their "consent" to exercise power. By using focus groups and elaborate polling techniques, those who design these messages are able to derive the only information they're interested in receiving *from* citizens—feedback useful in fine-tuning their efforts at manipulation.[2]

Such persuasion is not *always* unethical, because it often supports good and useful causes and might even be justified if challenged. But it is not inherently ethical either, because it sidesteps a careful consideration of supporting evidence and arguments. *It avoids the ethical burden of justification.*

There is another kind of persuasion that is part of the Western tradition reaching back over several thousand years to the speeches of Pericles and Demosthenes in ancient Greece. **Argumentative persuasion**, as we shall call it, builds arguments out of evidence and reasoning. It displays patterns of reasoning for critical inspection and asks for agreement and action. It is not *always* ethical, because evil speakers can sometimes twist evidence and disguise bad reasoning, deceiving even careful listeners. But it is inherently ethical, because it assumes the burden of justification, addresses our judgment rather than our impulses, and honors the intellectual behaviors that make us human.

Argumentative persuasion is the business of this chapter. We consider ways *to build powerful arguments that deserve respectful attention from thoughtful listeners.* We show how to develop evidence and proofs, build patterns of effective reasoning, and avoid defects of evidence, proof, and reasoning.

Developing Evidence

In Chapter 8, we explored the use of supporting materials. In persuasive speaking, these materials function as **evidence**, the foundation of ethical argument.

■ **Facts and figures are often the ultimate justification for asking us to believe or act in different ways.**[3] As we shall see, they can be especially important during the awareness phase of the persuasive process when they reveal a reality that calls for action. Recent research has confirmed the importance of statistical evidence in persuading others: Such evidence can be highly credible in our no-nonsense society.[4] Statistical knowledge becomes

---

manipulative persuasion Persuasion that works through suggestion, colorful images, music, and attractive spokespersons more than through evidence and reasoning. It avoids the ethical burden of justification.

argumentative persuasion Persuasion built on evidence and reasoning.

evidence Supporting materials used in persuasive speeches, including facts and figures, examples, narratives, and testimony.

embedded in our thinking and helps persuasion endure beyond the moment. This is why the corruption of such evidence, revealed recently in efforts to bribe scientists into reporting certain conclusions about global warming, threatens the integrity of public understanding and the communication based on it.[5]

■ **Examples can awaken feelings that make listeners want to act and can help bring factual situations into sharp focus.** One of the most memorable moments of the 2004 Democratic convention occurred when Ron Reagan, son of the late Republican president, urged the delegates to support embryonic stem cell research. To arouse sympathy for this cause, he developed an extended example:

> I know a child—well, she must be 13 now—I'd better call her a young woman. . . . She has memories. She has hopes. And she has juvenile diabetes.
>
> Like so many kids with this disease, she has adjusted amazingly well. The insulin pump she wears—she's decorated hers with rhinestones. She can insert her own catheter needle. She has learned to sleep through the blood drawings in the wee hours of the morning. She's very brave. She is also quite bright and understands full well the progress of her disease and what that might ultimately mean: blindness, amputation, diabetic coma. Every day, she fights to have a future.
>
> What excuse will we offer this young woman should we fail her now? What might we tell . . . the millions of others who suffer? That when given an opportunity to help, we turned away? That facing political opposition, we lost our nerve? That even though we knew better, we did nothing?[6]

This powerful example helped prepare Reagan's listeners emotionally for his final appeal.

The other great function of examples is to empower factual evidence by bringing situations into sharp, living focus for listeners. Whenever listeners ask, "Can you give me an example?" they are asking for this kind of clarification and authentication. Philanthropist Bill Gates, as he argued for reform in American high school education, used three key examples as evidence to prove his point that raised expectations can improve student performance. As he pointed to dramatic successes in Kansas, Rhode Island, and California, Gates built a compelling case in support of his argument.[7]

■ **Narratives can carry listeners to the scene of a problem and make them witnesses to a living drama.** Student speaker Kirsten Lientz illustrated this function when she opened a speech with the following narrative:

> It's a cold, icy December afternoon. You hear a distant crash, then screams, and finally the unending moan of a car horn fills the silence. You rush the short distance to the scene of the crash, where you find an SUV overturned with a young woman and two small boys inside. The woman and one of the boys climb from the wreckage unhurt; the other boy, however, is pinned between the dashboard and the roof of the car, unconscious and not breathing.
>
> Would you know what to do? Or would you stand there wishing you did? These events are real. Bob Flath saved this child with the skills he acquired at his company's first aid workshop.

After this dramatic narrative introduction, Kirsten's listeners were ready to listen to her speech urging them to take the first aid course offered at her university.

Recent research confirms that narratives can be a powerful form of evidence, perhaps because they are so vivid.[8] Moreover, when they are effective, examples and stories enjoy a special advantage in persuasion because listeners find them hard to argue with.[9] We can dispute the meaning of facts and figures, and even debate them. But a good example or story is hard to deny and lingers in memory.

■ **When you use testimony in a persuasive speech, you call on experts as witnesses to support your position.** Expert testimony is most effective when (1) the audience knows little about the issue because it is new or complicated; (2) listeners don't feel that the issue affects them directly; and/or (3) listeners lack the ability or motivation to analyze the situation independently.[10]

Introduce your witnesses carefully, pointing out their credentials. To support her call for air safety improvements, one of our students, Juli Pardell, cited eight authoritative sources of information. In his plea for organ donors, Paul Fowler, another student, cited four reputable books. It was not just Juli or Paul speaking—it was *all* these sources of testimony together, supporting the speaker's voice.

Witnesses who testify *against* their apparent self-interest are called **reluctant witnesses**. They provide some of the most powerful evidence available in persuasion. Democratic critics of President Clinton's personal behavior or Republican critics of President George W. Bush's foreign policies often had more impact because they appeared to be speaking against their political affiliations.

In ethical persuasive speaking, you should rely mainly on expert testimony. Use prestige or lay testimony as secondary sources of evidence. You can use prestige testimony to stress values you want listeners to embrace. You can use lay testimony to relate an issue to the lives of listeners. Keep in mind that when you quote others, you are associating yourself with them. Be careful with whom you associate!

As you search for evidence, keep an open mind. Consider different points of view, so that you don't simply present one perspective without being aware of others.

Ethics *Alert! 15.1*

Guidelines for the Ethical Use of Evidence

To earn a reputation for the ethical use of evidence, follow these rules:

1. Provide evidence from credible sources.

2. Identify your sources of evidence.

3. Use evidence that can be verified by experts.

4. Be sure such evidence has not been corrupted by outside interests.

5. Acknowledge disagreements among experts.

6. Do not withhold important evidence.

7. Use expert testimony to establish facts, prestige testimony to enhance credibility, and lay testimony to create identification.

8. Quote or paraphrase testimony accurately.

reluctant witnesses Witnesses who testify against their apparent self-interest.

Personal experience with a situation can qualify a speaker's testimony as was the case when former New York City mayor Rudy Giuliani testified before the 9/11 commission.

Gather more evidence than you think you will need so that you have a wide range from which to choose. Be sure you have facts, figures, or expert testimony for each of the major points you want to make. Use multiple sources and types of evidence to strengthen your case.

Developing Proofs

To build strong arguments, persuaders must develop powerful proofs. **Proofs** may be based on evidence, may tap into our emotional reactions, may be based on our social heritage, or may call on the personal leadership qualities of speakers in an effort to influence us.

The nature of proof has been studied since the Golden Age of Greece. In his *Rhetoric*, Aristotle identified three forms of proof. The first, **logos**, recognizes that we respond to reason. *At least we like to think that we are reasonable creatures.* When speeches make good sense to us, when they are grounded in strong evidence and move logically to the conclusions they want us to accept, we find them hard to resist.

The second, **pathos**, affirms that we can be touched by appeals to personal feelings such as fear, pity, and anger. Examples and narratives often provide the evidence this kind of proof emphasizes, just as Ron Reagan aroused both sympathy and indignation with his story of a 13-year-old girl fighting for her future against juvenile diabetes.

The third form, **ethos**, recognizes that we respond to our perceptions of a speaker's competence, character, goodwill, and dynamism. When these qualities seem positive, we *want* to agree with speakers. When these qualities seem negative or are lacking, speakers will have a hard time winning us over. We are also affected by the credibility of the evidence cited in a speech. If we respect the people you quote in your speech, we will listen respectfully to their testimony. If we are not impressed by them, you have created a problem for yourself.

In our time, the work of many scholars has confirmed the presence of a fourth dimension of proof, **mythos**, which suggests that we respond to appeals to the traditions and values of our culture and to the legends and folktales that embody them.[11] We are social beings who build much of our identity on our membership in groups, ranging from churches and universities to cities, states, and nations. If you can make a connection between your proposal and this social and cultural identity, listeners will give your ideas a careful hearing.

A persuasive speech rarely relies on a single kind of proof. Each type of proof brings its own coloration and strength to the fabric of persuasion. For this reason, perhaps, the traditional forms of proof are often discussed as though they were of equal importance to persuasion. But in manipulative persuasion, ethos, pathos, and mythos may be used more frequently than logos. Fast-food and automobile commercials rarely treat us as reasoning creatures.

On the other hand, argumentative persuasion stresses logos and assigns supporting roles to ethos, pathos, and mythos. Even if these latter forms of proof are vital in adding energy, color, and human interest to persuasion, they supplement the basic appeal to our rational nature. These priorities among the forms of proof are shown in Figure 15.2.

proof An interpretation of evidence that provides a good reason for listeners to agree with the speaker.

logos A form of proof that makes rational appeals based on facts and figures and expert testimony.

pathos Proof relying on appeals to emotions.

ethos A form of proof that relies on the audience's perceptions of a speaker's competence, character, good will, and dynamism.

Figure 15.2

Proof Priorities in Argumentative Persuasion

In the section that follows, we discuss ethos, pathos, and mythos as we build up to the consideration of logos. We discuss the strengths and qualities of these proofs so that you may weave them effectively into your own persuasive speech.

Proof by Ethos.   When you speak, listeners must sense that you are a person of strong conviction and that you know what you are talking about. Your sincerity and personal commitment must be beyond question. Listeners must feel that they can trust you—that you will not distort the truth for personal advantage. Ideally, they will also conclude that you are a likeable person who in turn likes them—that you are a person of goodwill.[12]

Clearly, listeners are strongly influenced by the credibility of speakers. Social scientists have discovered that credibility is a dynamic, not a stable quality: It can change during a speech.[13] As you stand to speak, listeners may already have some impressions of your character, ability, goodwill, and confidence. This is your **initial credibility** that you bring to a speech.

As you are actually speaking, your **emerging credibility** begins to build. We recall a student who, as a result of some very unpleasant speaking experiences before taking our class, suffered from acute communication apprehension. His nervousness caused him to read his first two speeches, speaking in a monotone and avoiding eye contact. It was hard to tell whether his speeches had good content because they were presented so poorly. We worked with him outside class, trying to build up his confidence. Finally, one day he broke through the wall he had built between himself and listeners. The process of his emerging credibility, as we experienced it that day, can be reconstructed in the following sequence of moments:

1. *Initial credibility* (as he rises to speak): We are smiling encouragement, but thinking to ourselves, "This is going to be painful."

2. "Well, he looks more comfortable. He is actually making eye contact! He is even smiling, and what a nice smile! Lights up the room."

3. "He clearly cares a lot about arts education. Didn't know he was capable of such feeling."

---

mythos A form of proof that connects a subject to the culture and tradition of a group of narratives.

initial credibility The audience's assessment of your ethos before you begin your speech.

emerging credibility The changes in the audience's assessment of ethos that occur as you present your speech.

Trustworthiness is an important dimension of proof by ethos. Former President Carter instills confidence when he speaks on humanitarian issues.

4. "Wow, he really knows his stuff. That's effective testimony, and impressive facts and statistics. Moving example too. The way he just used language—very good."

5. "That makes good sense. I'll go along with those recommendations."

6. (As the speech concluded in a congratulatory round of applause): "Well, we've got ourselves a speaker!"

The speaker's emerging credibility either changes or confirms initial credibility, resulting in your **terminal credibility**. Your terminal credibility when one speech concludes becomes your initial credibility when you present another.

As the example illustrates, the gap between initial and terminal credibility can be dramatic. The interesting thing is that more than the audience changed their assessment of credibility that day. The speaker had risen in his own estimation as well.

If you enjoy high ethos in the eyes of listeners, all your other proofs will be more effective as well. Your examples and stories will have more impact, and your facts and figures will be more believable. Even the words you use can be more intense and colorful, and such language itself can assure greater persuasive effects.[14] In sum, your personal ethos can be the key to whether you succeed or fail as a persuasive speaker.

The sources of information you cite in your speech provide another type of proof by ethos. Listeners also evaluate these sources in terms of their competence, character, goodwill, and power. If the evaluation of these sources is positive, audiences are more inclined to accept your position. Let's look at how student speaker Heide Nord used the ethos of her sources to help persuade her listeners to change their attitudes about suntanning. To support the claim "We should avoid prolonged exposure to the sun," Heide emphasized expert testimony backed up by lay testimony:

> The most recent *Consumer Report* of the Food and Drug Administration tells us, "Prolonged exposure to sunlight without protection is responsible for about 90 percent of skin cancer." The article describes the case of Wendell Scarberry, a skin cancer patient who has had over a hundred surgeries. Wendell talks about the seriousness of the disease and urges us to be careful about sun exposure. "You can't cure skin cancer," he says, "by just having the doc whack it off." Finally, the American Cancer Society, in its pamphlet *Fry Now Pay Later*, says that skin cancer most often occurs among people who spend a lot of time in the sun, especially if they have been overexposed during their teens or twenties. Well, that's where most of us are right now. The FDA, the American Cancer Society, and Mr. Scarberry speak loudly together, and we ought to listen to them.

Heidi's obvious commitment, together with the combination of expert and lay testimony, made her speech highly credible.

---

terminal credibility The audience's assessment of your ethos after you have made a presentation.

Proof based on the testimony of reliable, competent, and trustworthy sources is extremely important in persuasive speaking. *Identify your sources and point out why they are qualified to speak on the subject.* It is also helpful if you can say that the testimony is recent. For maximum effect, quote experts directly rather than paraphrasing them.

Proof by Pathos. People usually respond strongly when they feel angry, afraid, guilty, excited, or compassionate toward others. If used ethically in a context of argumentative persuasion, appeals to personal feelings can change bad attitudes or move people to act for good causes.[15]

When speakers tell personal stories, emotional appeals can be especially effective. Personal narratives blend the power of feeling with strong credibility. During a congressional debate on handgun control legislation, James Brady, the presidential press secretary who was shot during the assassination attempt on President Reagan, testified before the U.S. Senate Judiciary Subcommittee. Speaking from his wheelchair, he said:

> There was a day when I walked the halls of this Senate and worked closely with many of you and your staffs. There was a wonderful day when I was fortunate enough to serve the President of the United States in a capacity I had dreamed of all my life. And for a time, I felt that people looked up to me. Today, I can tell you how hard it is to have people speaking down to me. But nothing has been harder than losing the independence and control we all so value in life. I need help getting out of bed, help taking a shower, and help getting dressed.
>
> There are some who oppose a simple seven-day waiting period for handgun purchases because it would inconvenience gun buyers. Well, I guess I am paying for their convenience. And I am one of the lucky ones. I survived being shot through the head. Other shooting victims are not as fortunate.[16]

Often, appeals to emotions are the only way to convince people of the human dimensions of a problem or the need for immediate action. So how can you use proof by pathos effectively? Consider again the section on motivation in Chapter 5. Motives, you may recall, drive our behavior. We tend to become emotional when our motives are frustrated. Therefore, effective appeals to pathos often connect the speaker's points in personal ways with this underlying pattern of motives. Figure 15.3 illustrates how such connections might be made to relevant motives.

Figure 15.3

Connecting Pathos with Motives

Motives	Personal Emotions	Possible Connection
Health/Safety	Fear/Security	Does my subject affect the personal well-being and safety of listeners?
Nurturance/Altruism	Sympathy/Caring for others	Does my subject invite feelings of sympathy and benevolence for the fate of others?
Family/Significant Others	Love	Might my subject ignite feelings for loved ones?

The Western frontier is a major source of mythos in American speeches. *American Progress*, a painting by American artist John Gast, portrays many icons and ideographs. Which ones can you identify?

As powerful as emotional proof may be, it should be used with caution. If an appeal to feeling is too obvious, audiences may suspect you are trying to manipulate them. Appeals to negative emotions such as fear or guilt are especially tricky because they can boomerang, causing listeners to discredit both you and your speech. When you use appeals to feeling, justify them with solid evidence. In your presentation, let your voice and body language understate rather than overstate the emotional appeal. Don't engage in theatrics.

Proof by Mythos.   Appeals to the values, faith, and feelings that make up our social identity can be a powerful source of proof. Such appeals, often expressed in traditional stories, sayings, and symbols, assume that audiences value their membership in a culture and share its heritage. Communication scholar Martha Solomon Watson has noted, "Rhetoric which incorporates mythical elements taps into rich cultural reservoirs."[17]

Appeals to cultural identity often call on patriotism and remind us of our heroes or enemies. They may gain power from political narratives, such as the story of George Washington's harsh winter at Valley Forge. Or they may be embedded in folk sayings, as when speakers remind us that ours is "the land of opportunity."[18] Appeals to mythos also may be grounded in economic legends, such as American stories of success through hard work and thrift that celebrate the rise to power from humble beginnings. Such stories justify economic power in our society while assuring the powerless that they too can make it if only they have "the right stuff."

Appeals to cultural identity may also draw on religious narratives. Sacred documents, such as the Bible, provide a rich storehouse of parables, used not only in sermons but also in political speeches.[19] For example, references to the Good Samaritan are often used to justify government efforts to help those who are in need.

Stories need not be retold in their entirety each time they are invoked. Because they are so familiar, allusions to them may be sufficient. The culturetypes discussed in Chapter 12 are often called into service, because they compress myths into a few provocative words. Words like *progress, science,* and *education* have positive mythic overtones, and *terrorist, pollution,* and *weapons of mass destruction* are negatively charged. In his speech accepting the Democratic presidential nomination in 1960, John F. Kennedy called on the myth of the American frontier to move Americans to action:

> The New Frontier of which I speak is not a set of promises—it is a set of challenges. It sums up not what I intend to offer the American people, but what I intend to ask of them.[20]

This appeal to cultural identity emerged as a central theme of Kennedy's presidency. He didn't need to refer directly to the legends of Daniel Boone and Davy Crockett or to the tales of the Oregon Trail to meet the challenges that lay ahead—he was able to conjure up those thoughts with the phrase "the New Frontier."

How can you use proof by mythos in a classroom speech? Once again, we return to the earlier discussion of motivation in Chapter 5. The social motives discussed there, which tend to engage group emotions, may also suggest guides to the development of proof by mythos. Figure 15.4 shows how connections might be made between mythos and motives.

Let's see how Robert Owens used such appeals to urge stronger action against drug traffic in urban slums. Robert wanted to establish that "we must win the battle against drugs on the streets of America." He supported this statement by creating a sense of outrage in listeners over the betrayal of the American dream in urban America:

> Read the latest issue of *Time* magazine, and you'll meet an America you never sang about in the songs you learned in school. It's an America in which hope, faith, and dreams are nothing but a bitter memory.
>
> They call America a land of hope, but it's hard to hope when your mother is a cocaine addict on Susquehanna Avenue in North Philadelphia.
>
> They call America a land of faith, but what faith can you cling to when even God seems to have abandoned the street corners to the junkies and the dealers!
>
> They call America a land of dreams, but what kind of dreams can you have when all you hear at night as you lie in bed are the curses and ranting of buyers and dealers.
>
> We might be able to redeem the hope, the faith, and the dreams Americans like to talk about. But we have to do more than just declare war on drugs. We've got to *go* to war, and we've got to win! If we don't, the crack in the Liberty Bell may only symbolize a deadly drug that is destroying the American spirit all over this land.

These appeals to a betrayed mythos justified Robert's concluding plea for a broad-based, aggressive campaign to rid America of its drug culture. *The unique function of appeals to cultural identity is to help listeners understand how the speaker's*

Figure 15.4

Connecting Mythos with Motives

Motives	Group Emotion	Possible Connection
Maintain Control/ Stability	Respect for/love of tradition	Does my proposal reaffirm traditions that my listeners want to protect?
Honor Affiliations	Feelings of group pride/patriotism	Does my subject connect with audience feelings of loyalty to a group and pride in membership?
Preserve Group Identity	Respect for heroes/great deeds	Does my speech connect with models of heroism and memories of great events? Does my speech call upon values that are vital to group identity?

Speaker's Notes **15.1**

When and How to Use Proof

As you decide how to align your proofs for maximum effectiveness, follow these guidelines:

1. To increase awareness and understanding, use rational appeals based on facts, statistics, and expert testimony *(logos)*.

2. To communicate the human dimensions of a problem, stir listeners with moving examples and stories *(pathos)*.

3. To reassure listeners that you are a credible speaker, convince them that you know what you are talking about,

that you are fair and honest, and that you have audience interests at heart *(ethos)*.

4. To connect a problem with group culture, show how it relates to popular traditions, legends, and symbols *(mythos)*.

recommendations fit into the total belief and value patterns of their group. An appeal that accomplishes this goal gives such proof a special role in the persuasive process we discuss in Chapter 16. It can help integrate new attitudes and action into the group's culture.

Like appeals to personal feeling, appeals to cultural identity can be a great good or a considerable evil. At their best, such appeals heighten our appreciation of who we are *as a people* and promote consistency between cultural values and public policy. However, when misused, these appeals can make it seem that there is only *one legitimate culture.* Some of those who argued for introducing democratic government to Iraq and the Middle East seemed to base their arguments on the United States model. To the extent they implied that our system is superior to all other options, no matter what the circumstances, they may have been guilty of abusing the appeal to mythos. Also, certain appeals to cultural identity can abuse those who choose not to conform to the dominant values or those who belong to marginalized cultural and religious groups, such as Latinos or Muslims. Such appeals can tear apart the social fabric of our society, and even of our world.

Patterns of Reasoning

A persuasive speech that is effective may activate the power of ethos, pathos, and mythos. Yet these proofs are all secondary to the central focus of ethical persuasion: proof by logos. Thoughtful listeners must be convinced by the patterns of reasoning you develop in your speech. Such listeners will apply the following critical tests:

- Have central issues and terms been clearly and fairly defined?

- Does the speech reason from sound principles?

- Is the speech firmly anchored in reality?

- Does the speech reason acceptably from similar or parallel cases?

In the sections that follow, we consider each of these tests, explain its meaning, and indicate how you might pass it successfully.

Definitions of Central Concepts

The Greek philosopher Socrates was one of the first to insist that ethical persuasion begins with a clear understanding of the meanings of important terms. Have you ever had a heated discussion with someone, only to discover later that the two of you were not even talking about the same thing? If speakers and listeners don't share such understanding from the outset, it is difficult to communicate. When the speaker and audience come from different backgrounds, careful definitions are even more important. Opening his speech on "gender bending," Brandon Rader was careful to offer the following definition: "If you are a gender bender, you dress or act or think or talk like people in your community assume someone of the opposite sex would do or act or talk or dress." Having shared this understanding, Brandon went on to argue that most assumptions about gender benders are quite wrong. Definitions like Brandon's take a term that may be unfamiliar to many audience members and translate it into simpler, more familiar language.

Not all definitions involve translating technical language into familiar terms. Some of the most interesting definitions offered by speakers are efforts to change listeners' perspectives so that they will be more sympathetic to the arguments that will follow. Should alcohol be defined as a drug? Should a fetus be defined as a human being? Definitions that affirm or deny such questions can prepare the way for elaborate arguments advocating different kinds of public policy.

In the 1968 Memphis sanitation strike that led to the assassination of Dr. Martin Luther King Jr., the workers marched carrying signs that read, "I Am a Man." This simple definitional statement was actually the tip of a complex underlying moral argument. The strikers were claiming they had *not* been treated like men in social, political, and economic terms.

Dr. Richard Corlin, former president of the American Medical Association, used many types of evidence in his speech on gun violence. His use of analogy was especially striking.

An especially interesting effort to redefine perspectives occurred in a speech by Richard Corlin, president of the American Medical Association, at the 2001 AMA annual meeting (see his speech at the end of this chapter). Alarmed over the rise in gun-related fatalities, Dr. Corlin wanted to redefine gun violence in America as a "public health crisis." Here is the section near the beginning of his speech in which he introduces this attempted change of perspectives:

> With the preponderance of weapons these days, it comes as no surprise that gun violence—both self-inflicted and against others—is now a serious public health crisis. No one can avoid its brutal and ugly presence. No one. Not physicians. Not the public. And most certainly—not the politicians—no matter how much they might want to.[21]

Having introduced a perspective that was no doubt novel for many members of his audience, Dr. Corlin went on build extensive arguments to support it. By the end of his speech, the "public health crisis" he had identified near the opening of his speech had evolved into a "uniquely American epidemic." As these examples make clear, definitions can be *the fundamental issues at the heart of controversies.* If you attempt to redefine your audience's perspective on a subject, you may have to defend your effort with all the evidence, proof, and credibility you can muster.

Reasoning from Principle

As we absorb the folkways of our culture, we acquire principles that guide the way we think and live. For example "freedom of speech" is written into the Constitution of the United States as a principle of government.

When we **reason from principle**, we use such guides to justify our value judgments and calls to action. Such reasoning is sometimes called **deductive**, because it deduces from some general principle a conclusion about a particular relevant case. Consider a hypothetical example. A speaker begins by reminding listeners of a principle she believes they all accept: "We all believe in freedom of speech." In logical terms, such a principle is known as the **major premise**. Next, the speaker relates a specific issue to that principle, creating what is called the **minor premise**: "Melvin would like to speak." Finally, the speaker reaches her **conclusion**: "We should let Melvin speak." Because of their respect for the principle expressed in the major premise, many listeners would nod assent, even though they might not particularly like Melvin.

When this pattern of major premise/minor premise/conclusion occurred in persuasion about public issues, Aristotle called it the **enthymeme**. He described enthymemes as vital in the persuasion of everyday life. Indeed, he said, they are the most important rhetorical resource. In his 2003 State of the Union address, President Bush developed a major premise that justified conclusions ranging from a massive program to relieve AIDS in Africa to a threat to invade Iraq. Here is what he said:

> The American flag stands for more than our power and our interests. Our founders dedicated this country to the cause of human dignity, the rights of every person and the possibilities of every life. This conviction leads us into the world to help the afflicted, and defend the peace, and confound the designs of evil men.[22]

Because it begins by reminding listeners of shared values, reasoning from principle is useful for establishing common ground with reluctant audiences. Such reasoning can also point out inconsistencies between beliefs and behaviors—the gap between what we practice and what we preach. For example, if you can show that the censorship of song lyrics is inconsistent with freedom of speech, then you will have presented a good reason for people to condemn such censorship. *We are more likely to change a practice that is inconsistent with cherished principles or values than we are to change the principles or values.* Because people like to be consistent and maintain the integrity of their values, reasoning from principle becomes a powerful way to achieve harmony among attitudes, beliefs, and values.

Occasionally, the pattern of reasoning in an enthymeme is not entirely visible in a speech. For example, the major premise may not be stated: Speakers may simply assume that the principle it expresses is already accepted by listeners. When offered appropriate cues, listeners will think of these principles and complete the

reasoning from principle Argumentative reasoning that is based upon shared principles, values, and rules, sometimes called deductive reasoning.

deductive reasoning Arguing from a general principle to a specific case.
major premise The statement of a general principle on which an argument is based.

minor premise The statement of a specific instance that relates to the general principle on which an argument is based.

speaker's line of thought on their own. As she spoke of the problems of Native Americans, Ashley Roberson spent much of her time demonstrating the reality of "social injustice on reservations," which functioned as the minor premise in her enthymeme. She did not think it necessary to state the implied major premise, "Social injustice in the United States should not be tolerated." Instead, she felt justified in concluding, "We must eradicate social injustice on reservations." As she indicted the School of the Americas, Amanda Miller concentrated on demonstrating that the school had been training terrorists. She did not think it necessary to state the major premise, "The United States should try to end terrorism, not perpetuate it." Instead, she felt justified in drawing her conclusion, "We ought to close the School of the Americas now."

We should realize, however, that not all members of the audience might accept principles that seem to us beyond question. For example, some researchers have discovered that if you read the Bill of Rights to people without telling them it is part of the United States Constitution, an alarming percentage will describe it as "radical" or "communistic." Therefore, you should not take such principles for granted. You may have to explain and defend them to reinforce your listeners' belief in them. You may need to reawaken faith in the principles by telling stories or offering examples that demonstrate their value.

Another point critical to such reasoning comes when a speaker tries to show that a condition or situation—the minor premise—actually exists. People may not argue passionately about the *principle* of environmental protection, but assertions about a specific case of pollution can generate a good deal of heat. Your persuasive efforts may have to focus on that issue, emphasizing the kind of reasoning we discuss in the next section.

As you develop a principled pattern of reasoning for your speech, keep these cautions in mind:

- **Be certain your audience will accept the major premises on which your arguments are based.** Remind listeners why they believe as they do. Cite prestige sources who testify to the importance of such faith. Use appeals to feeling and to cultural identity to reinforce the principles. Use rational appeals to show their practical importance.

- **Demonstrate the existence of relevant conditions.** This, as we shall see in the next section, is where empirical reasoning joins with principled reasoning to build convincing arguments.

- **Explain the relationship between principles and conditions (the major and minor premises).** Don't expect your audience to get the point automatically. Listeners may not see the connection between their responsibility to maintain the natural beauty of their country and specific environmental conditions that need reform. Help them by drawing the point explicitly.

- **Be certain your reasoning is free from flaws and fallacies.** We discuss such problems of argument in the final section of this chapter.

- **Be sure your conclusion offers a clear direction for listeners.** Don't leave them foundering without a clear idea as to what you want them to do.

Reasoning from Reality

Persuasive speakers must have an accurate grasp of the situation they are discussing. **Reasoning from reality** depends either on the speaker's personal experience or on

---

conclusion The ending of the speech, which summarizes the message and leaves listeners with something to remember. Also, the final statement of

the relationship between the major and minor premises of an argument.
enthymeme Pattern of deductive reasoning as it occurs in persuasion about public issues.

reasoning from reality Emphasis on factual evidence in guiding one's general conclusions and decisions.

Speaker's Notes **15.2**

Reasoning from Principle

Let your reasoning from principle follow these procedures:

1. If there is any doubt, remind listeners why they honor the principles from which you reason.

2. Demonstrate that the conditions relevant to the principle you invoke actually exist.

3. Show how these conditions and principles are related and why that relationship requires action.

4. Check for flaws in your reasoning.

5. Make it easy for listeners to enact what you advance.

knowledge provided by experts. This knowledge is reflected in the facts, statistics, examples, and testimony used in the speech. Reasoning from reality is sometimes called **inductive** because it draws general conclusions from particular instances. Inductive reasoning is the classic method of scientific investigation, and science remains a "god term" for many listeners in our culture:[23] if you can show that "science supports my argument," you will have strengthened your case for most audiences. Again, for this reason, the abuse of scientific evidence, attempted when so-called "think tanks" offer financial inducements to scientists to reach certain predetermined conclusions, is an ominous practice in a society that depends on the integrity of public deliberation.[24]

Dr. Richard Corlin, in his presidential address before the American Medical Association on gun violence, was uniquely positioned to speak both from direct personal experience and as a careful observer of the work of other experts. In the section that follows, we can see how he reasons from reality, citing statistic after statistic and example after example, using contrast to highlight the force of his evidence. Note also how he speaks *as a scientist addressing other scientists:*

> In 1993 and 1994, we resolved that the AMA would, among other actions, "support scientific research and objective discussion aimed at identifying causes of and solutions to the crime and violence problem." Scientific research and objective discussion because we as physicians are—first and foremost—scientists. We need to look at the science of the subject, the data, and—if you will—the micro-data, before we make a diagnosis. Not until then can we agree upon the prognosis or decide upon a course of treatment.
>
> First, let's go straight to the science that we do know. How does this disease present itself? Since 1962, more than a million Americans have died in firearm suicides, homicides, and unintentional injuries. In 1998 alone, 30,708 Americans died by gunfire:
>
> - 17,424 in firearm suicides
> - 12,102 in firearm homicides
> - 866 in unintentional shootings
>
> Also in 1998, more than 64,000 people were treated in emergency rooms for nonfatal firearm injuries.

inductive reasoning Reasoning from specific factual instances to reach a general conclusion.

This is a uniquely American epidemic. In the same year that more than 30,000 people were killed by guns in America, the number in Germany was 1,164; in Canada, it was 1,034; in Australia, 391; in England and Wales, 211; and in Japan, the number for the entire year was 83.[25]

Although reasoning from principle and reasoning from reality may seem quite different, they actually work together. Reasoning from reality can reinforce principles so that they don't appear to be simply items of blind faith. For example, if we can demonstrate empirically that "free and open discussion actually results in better public decisions," then we bring both morality and practicality to the support of freedom of speech.

Reasoning from reality is critical for demonstrating the truth of the minor premise in an enthymeme. Is the censorship of song lyrics an actual threat, or is it merely some bogeyman in the minds of liberals? Again, testimony from those who wish to censor and who have the power to censor would authenticate the threat. Similarly, Ashley Roberson had to prove with facts, statistics, and examples that the problems existing on Native American reservations were of such magnitude that they constituted "social injustice." Clearly, reasoning from reality can empower reasoning from principle in persuasive speeches, and the two forms are often found woven together.

Reasoning from reality also implies an understanding of cause–effect relationships. In his speech on gun violence, once Dr. Corlin had described the magnitude of the problem, he went on to explore its causes. One such cause pinpointed the culture of violence accessible to young children through video games. As he put it:

The spread of gun-related injuries and death is especially tragic when it involves our children. Like young lungs and tar and nicotine—young minds are especially responsive to the deadliness of gun violence.

Lieutenant Colonel Dave Grossman, a West Point professor of psychology and military science, has documented how video games act as killing simulators, teaching our children not just to shoot—but to kill. Grossman, who calls himself an expert in "killology," cites as evidence the marksmanship of the two children, aged 11 and 13, in the Jonesboro, Arkansas, shootings in 1998. Both shooters were avid video game players. And just like in a video game—they fired off 27 shots—and hit 15 people. Killing four of their fellow students—and a teacher. Such deadly accuracy is rare and hard to achieve—even by well-trained police and military marksmen.[26]

As you incorporate reasoning from reality into your arguments, keep in mind these basic requirements:

- You must be objective enough to see the situation clearly. Do not let your biases warp your perceptions. Look at an issue from as many perspectives as possible.

- You must compile a sufficient number of observations. One or two isolated incidents cannot justify reality claims.

- Since situations surrounding relevant issues are constantly changing, you must be sure your observations are up to date.

- Your observations must be truly representative of the situation. The exception does not prove the rule.

Speaker's Notes 15.3

Reasoning from Reality

To ground your reasoning in reality, satisfy the following tests:

1. Are your observations objective?

2. Have you observed enough?

3. Are your observations recent?

4. Are your observations representative of the situation?

5. Do your observations adequately justify your conclusion?

6. Have you read widely enough to see if experts agree?

7. If experts disagree, will you acknowledge their disagreement and explain and defend your preferences among them?

8. Have you verified your experts' credentials so you can present them in your speech?

- Your observations must actually justify your conclusion. They must be relevant to the claim you wish to demonstrate.

- If your inductive exposure comes from library or Internet research, don't just accept the testimony of the first expert you encounter. Read more widely to see whether experts agree with each other, and if they disagree, decide which of them are most credible. Be prepared to justify and defend your evaluation of evidence in your speech.

- As you present facts, statistics, examples, and testimony, be sure to introduce the experts who are the sources of the evidence. Establish their credentials to reassure thoughtful listeners. Beginning speakers often neglect this important requirement of successful persuasion.

Reasoning from Parallel Cases

When we deal with a problem by considering a similar situation and drawing lessons from it, we are **reasoning from parallel cases**. Such **analogical reasoning**, as it is sometimes called, can be useful to frame an unfamiliar, abstract, or difficult problem in terms of something that is more familiar, more concrete, or more easily understood. It also can be used to dramatize the speaker's claim: "If we don't deal with global warming, our children will inherit a degraded environment. Just like the tiger and the elephant, our habitat is in crisis."

Dr. Corlin used a vivid analogy to underscore the importance of video games in acclimating susceptible young minds into America's culture of gun violence. Reasoning from parallel cases helped him both magnify the problem and bring it into the understanding of listeners:

> I want you to imagine with me a computer game called "Puppy Shoot." In this game, puppies run across the screen. Using a joystick, the game player aims a gun that shoots the puppies. The player is awarded one point for a flesh wound, three points for a body shot, and ten points for a head shot. Blood spurts out each time a puppy is hit—and brain tissue splatters all over whenever there's a head shot. The dead puppies pile up at the bottom of the screen. When the shooter gets to 1,000 points, he gets to exchange his pistol for an Uzi, and the point values go up.

reasoning from parallel cases Presenting a similar situation and how it was handled as the basis of an argument. Often called analogical reasoning.

analogical reasoning Creating a strategic perspective on a subject by relating it to something similar about which the audience has strong feelings.

If a game as disgusting as that were to be developed, every animal rights group in the country, along with a lot of other organizations, would protest, and there would be all sorts of attempts made to get the game taken off the market. Yet, if you just change puppies to people in the game I described, there are dozens of them already on the market—sold under such names as "Blood Bath," "Psycho Toxic," "Redneck Rampage," and "Soldier of Fortune."[27]

As useful as analogical reasoning can be in dramatizing arguments, it can be even more useful in persuading listeners to accept solutions. For example, in the continuing debate over our nation's drug policy, those who favor legalizing "recreational" drugs frequently base their arguments on an analogy to Prohibition.[28] They claim that the Prohibition amendment caused more problems than it solved because it made drinking an adventure and led to the rise of a criminal empire. They then claim that our efforts to outlaw recreational drugs have had the same result. The reason, they say, is that it is impossible to ban a human desire—that to try to do so simply encourages contempt for the law. Moreover, they assert that legalizing drugs would help put the international drug dealers out of business, just as the repeal of Prohibition helped bring about the downfall of the gangsters of the 1930s. Finally, they argue, if drug sales were legal, it would be easier to control the quality of drugs, thus reducing the danger to users (parallel to the health problems associated with bootleg whiskey during Prohibition).

As this example shows, analogical reasoning emphasizes strategic points of comparison between similar situations. People on both sides of an issue will focus on these points, using evidence and proofs to defend or attack them. Opponents to legalizing drugs claim that there are many important differences between drugs and alcohol.[29] They say that alcohol is not as addictive for casual users as heroin or cocaine. They contend that legalization would multiply the drug problem, not reduce it, because it would make drugs more accessible and make them seem acceptable. They further suggest that since many drug abusers are prone to violence, the cost to society would increase. Thus, the public debate rages on over these crucial points of comparison.

What makes analogical reasoning work? It is similar to empirical reasoning from reality in that it seeks insight through careful observation. Analogy, however, concentrates *on one similar situation* rather than ranging across many. This means that although analogical reasoning may seem more concrete and interesting than some forms of inductive reasoning (such as that based often on statistical evidence), it can also be less reliable. Before you decide to develop an analogy as part of your argument, be sure that the important similarities outweigh the dissimilarities. If you must strain to make an analogy fit, rely on other forms of reasoning.

Speaker's Notes 15.4

Developing Powerful Arguments

To build arguments that will influence thoughtful listeners, follow these guidelines:

1. Provide clear definitions of basic terms.

2. Justify arguments by reasoning from accepted principles.

3. Remind listeners of why they honor these principles.

4. Convince listeners that your arguments are based in reality.

5. Create a vivid sense of problems.

6. Use a similar situation as a model from which to draw comparisons that illustrate and favor your position.

7. Build arguments to answer questions reasonable listeners might ask.

The Interplay of Reasoning

Patterns of reasoning often interact in persuasive speeches. One model that displays this interaction was developed by Stephen Toulmin, a British logician.[30] The Toulmin model (see Figure 15.5) includes six elements: data, claim, warrant, backing, reservations, and qualifier.

Data.   Facts, statistics, examples, and expert testimony constitute **data** in the Toulmin model. By featuring the importance of data, the model emphasizes the role of inductive reasoning. Dr. Richard Corlin established a rich array of data in his speech, "The Secrets of Gun Violence in America." Similarly, Josh Logan's speech, "Global Burning," reprinted in Appendix B, presented a range of data to justify his arguments.

Claim.   The **claim** is the conclusion the speaker draws from the data. Dr. Corlin wanted his audience of physicians to accept his claim that gun violence in America is an epidemic that demands a search for cures. Josh wanted us to accept his claim that controlling global warming is a personal, national, and international imperative.

Warrant.   The **warrant** supplies the principle that justifies the movement from data to claim. It functions like a major premise and represents the role of deductive reasoning in the model. Dr. Corlin's speech began by establishing a critical definition: *Gun violence is an epidemic and therefore a medical emergency.* His warrant, which he leaves audience members to draw on their own, might be reconstructed: *Whenever an epidemic exists, physicians—by the nature of their calling—must seek remedies and cures.* Those who accepted this warrant might feel compelled to accept the claim: *The AMA should initiate an aggressive campaign to find cures for gun violence in America.*

Similarly, in Josh's speech concerning the legitimacy of global warming, the warrant might be reconstructed as follows: *Whenever hundreds of scientists, working independently in countries around the globe, come to the same or similar conclusions, we can rely on the results.* Listeners who affirmed this warrant should also then accept the claim: *We must accept the reality of global warming.*

Toulmin's model can also supply a warrant for the use of analogical reasoning in argument. That warrant might be stated as follows: *Whenever a parallel case*

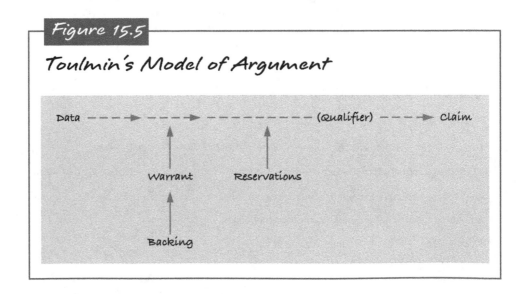

Figure 15.5

Toulmin's Model of Argument

Data - - - → - - - → - - - - - - - (Qualifier) - - - → Claim

Warrant   Reservations

Backing

---

data The factual evidence in an argument as featured in the Toulmin model.

claim The conclusion the speaker draws based on the data in an argument. Also, conclusions that go beyond factual statements to make judgments about their subjects.

warrant The principle that justifies moving from data to claim in an argument.

presents a set of compelling similarities to the subject we are discussing, and no significant dissimilarities exist, we can draw a relevant claim about our subject. We have seen how Dr. Corlin used a hypothetical analogy—the game he called "Puppy Shoot"—to dramatize the danger of the culture of violence encouraged by computer games.

Backing.   Occasionally, critical listeners or opponents may question the warrant. At such moments, you can defend the warrant by introducing support for it, called *backing*. Dr. Corlin anticipated that critics might question the activism in his implied warrant, so he introduced backing into his speech:

> We, as physicians, and as the American Medical Association, have an ethical and moral responsibility to do this—as our mission statement says—"to promote the science and art of medicine and the betterment of public health." If removing the scourge of gun violence isn't bettering the public health—what is?[31]

Thus, he defends his warrant in advance of attacks by citing the AMA mission statement as backing. Similarly, had anyone questioned Joshua's warrant, he could have pointed to past international research efforts on dread diseases to back his principle that when scientists agree on a global scale, one can rely on their conclusions.

Reservations.   Reservations acknowledge conditions under which the claim may not follow. Ethical persuaders have an obligation to inform listeners of such conditions, and thoughtful listeners will appreciate their candor. Not acknowledging legitimate reservations risks real damage to one's ethos should a critical listener point them out.

When conditions do create an element of uncertainty, reservations are signaled by the word *unless*. Josh might have introduced a reservation had he added, "Unless anyone can show that all these scientists were somehow mistaken, or in some sort of conspiracy, we must accept the ominous reality of global warming." Josh felt no need to acknowledge any such reservation.

Ethics *Alert! 15.2*

Building Ethical Arguments

To earn your reputation as an ethical persuader, observe the following guidelines:

1. Emphasize logical reasoning built on facts, statistics, and expert testimony.

2. Always supplement proof by pathos with hard evidence.

3. Never allow proof by mythos to become a mask for intolerance or an excuse to attack the rights of individuals who resist group values and culture.

4. Test the ethics of any persuasive strategy by considering how it will be judged by a thoughtful listener.

5. Strive to maintain consistency among attitudes, beliefs, values, and actions.

6. Acknowledge conditions that might disprove your argument.

7. As you research a problem, keep an open mind so that you can understand the various sides in a dispute.

Qualifiers.   Qualifiers are terms that address the force of the claim, taking into account possible reservations. Qualifiers often appear in such terms as *probably*, *almost certainly*, and *in all likelihood*. Dr. Corlin acknowledged no reservations in his speech, so he does not qualify the strength of his claim. Likewise, Josh was confident of the power of his data and the certainty of his claim concerning global warming, so he also did not use qualifiers.

You can use Toulmin's model of argument either as a critical template to help you become a more thoughtful listener or to gain an overview of your own reasoning processes in a speech you are designing. In the latter case, you may be able to identify any weak points during preparation and correct them before you make your presentation.

Avoiding Defective Persuasion

*I*t takes a lot of work to prepare a persuasive speech—analyzing your audience, researching your topic, planning your strategy, and developing powerful arguments that will convince judicious listeners. Do not ruin all your hard work by committing **fallacies**, or errors of reasoning. Fallacies may crop up in the evidence you use, the proofs you develop, or the reasoning in your arguments. There are also fallacies particular to some speech designs. In this section, we identify some of these major errors so that you can guard against them, both as speaker and as listener.

Defective Evidence

Evidence is defective if the speaker misuses facts, statistics, or testimony, or uses evidence inappropriately.

The evidence used in a persuasive speech must be representative of the situation.

Misuse of Facts.   The **slippery slope fallacy** assumes that once something happens, it will establish an irreversible trend leading to disaster. The slippery slope fallacy often involves oversimplification and outlandish hyperbole. For example, a prominent religious leader once suggested that feminism was "a socialist, antifamily political movement that encourages women to leave their husbands, kill their children, practice witchcraft, destroy capitalism, and become lesbians."[32] In the slippery slope fallacy, it is not logic but rather our darkest fears that drive the prediction of events.

A second misuse of facts involves the **confusion of fact and opinion**. A factual statement is objective and verifiable, such as "Most Republican governors support the lowering of taxes." An opinion is a personal interpretation of information: a statement of belief, feeling, attitude, or value. Normally, factual and opinion statements stay in their proper places. The problem comes when speakers make impassioned claims based on opinions, such as "The Republicans have done it now! They're violating our Constitution. They're tossing children out into the cold. They're depriving retired people

---

fallacies   Errors in reasoning that make persuasion unreliable.

slippery slope fallacy   The assumption that once something happens, an inevitable trend is established that will lead to disastrous results.

confusion of fact and opinion   A misuse of evidence in which personal opinions are offered as though they were facts, or facts are dismissed as though they were opinion.

of their right to a secure old age. These are the *facts* of what they're doing." Opinions can be useful in persuasive speeches when they represent careful interpretations that are supported by evidence. However, treating an opinion as a fact, or a fact as an opinion, is the source of many problems. It can make you seem to claim too much or too little and can raise questions about your competence and ethics.

At one time, hunters used to distract their dogs from a trail by dragging a smoked herring across it. In our time, the **red herring fallacy** occurs when persuaders try to draw attention away from the real issues in a dispute, perhaps because they feel vulnerable on those issues or because they see a chance to vilify the opposition. Often, the "red herring" they use is some sensational allegation. In the ongoing abortion controversy, some pro-choice advocates tried to discredit their opponents by associating them with terrorists, assassins, and bombers. In return, some pro-life advocates tried to smear their opposition by suggesting that abortion clinics were underwritten by "mafia money." Such charges from both sides divert attention from the central issues of the controversy.

Statistical Fallacies.   Audiences are often intimidated by numbers. We've all been taught that "figures don't lie" without being reminded that "liars figure." Speakers can exploit this tendency by creating statistical deceptions. For example, consider the **myth of the mean**. If you've ever vacationed in the mountains, you know that a stream may have an "average depth" of six inches, yet a person could drown in one of its deep pools. A speaker could tell you not to worry about poverty in Plattsville because the average income is well above the poverty level. Yet this average could be skewed by the fact that a few families are very wealthy, creating an illusion of well-being that is not true for most people. Averages are useful to summarize statistical information, but be sure they do not mask the reality of a situation.

Another statistical fallacy occurs when we offer **flawed statistical comparisons** that start from unequal bases. Suppose you have two salespersons, George and John, working for you. George has just opened a new account, giving him a total of two sales. John has opened three new accounts for a total of thirteen. George comes to you and asks for a promotion, arguing, "My success rate this year rose by 100 percent, while John's rose only 30 percent." George would be guilty of fallacious reasoning, if not bad salesmanship.

Defective Testimony.   Testimony can be misused in many different ways. Speakers may omit *when* a statement was made to hide the fact that the testimony is dated. They may leave out important facts about their experts, intimidating us with titles in statements such as "*Dr.* Michael Jones reported that smoking does not harm health." What the speaker *didn't* reveal was that Dr. Jones was a marketing professor who was writing public relations material for the Tobacco Growers Association. Speakers also abuse testimony when they cite words out of context that are not representative of a person's actual position. This can happen when a qualifier is presented as though it represented a concession, misquoting a statement such as "unless the growers are no longer using herbicides" as "Ah hah! He admits—and I quote him—'growers are no longer using herbicides.'" As we noted in Chapter 8, prestige and lay testimony can be misused if they replace expert opinion when facts must be established. Finally, the "voice of the people" can be easily misrepresented, depending on *which* people you choose to quote.

---

red herring fallacy The use of irrelevant material to divert attention.
myth of the mean The deceptive use of statistical averages in speeches.

flawed statistical comparisons Statistical reasoning that offers fallacious conclusions by comparing unequal or unlike situations.

InterConnections.
LearnMore 15.2

Fallacies

Fallacy Files

http://fallacyfiles.org

> *An interactive site containing an extensive collection of fallacies and bad argument, with definitions and examples; well organized and entertaining as well as educational (see especially "Stalking the Wild Fallacy"); developed by Gary N. Curtis.*

Watch Out for these Common Fallacies

www.coping.org/write/percept/fallacies/content.htm

> *Offers good discussion and often striking examples of fallacies in everyday reasoning; developed by James J. Messina and Constance M. Messina.*

Soyouwanna Avoid Common Logical Errors?

www.soyouwanna.com/site/syws/logic/logic.html

> *Discusses the logical rules that govern the making and evaluation of arguments from a philosophical perspective.*

Fallacies Drawn from Aristotle's *Rhetoric*

www.cc.utah.edu/~sms5/wrtg3700/bgtexts/fallacies.htm#Appeals

> *A discussion of common fallacies as they are developed in Aristotle's* Rhetoric, *one of the first books on public communication and perhaps the greatest.*

Inappropriate Evidence.   Other abuses occur when speakers deliberately use one form of evidence when they should be using another. For example, you might use facts and figures when examples would bring us closer to the human truth of a situation. Welfare statistics are sometimes misused in this way. When a speaker talks about poverty in terms of abstract numbers only, it distances listeners from the human reality of the problem. George Orwell once complained that such language "falls upon the [truth] like soft snow, blurring the outlines and covering up all the details."[33] On the other hand, speakers may use examples to arouse emotions when what is needed is the dispassionate picture provided by facts and figures. Testimony is abused when it is used to compensate for inadequate facts. Narratives that create mythos may also be used inappropriately. Calling someone a "Robin Hood who steals from the rich and gives to the poor" has been used to justify more than one crime.

Defective Proof

Any element of proof can be defective. We have already pointed out the danger when appeals to feelings overwhelm judgment and cloud the issue. Speakers might also misuse appeals to cultural identity to promote intolerance, such as "When are Native Americans going to start being *good* Americans?"

Similarly, speakers may abuse appeals to credibility by attacking the person instead of the problem. This is called an **ad hominem fallacy**. Such persuaders try to avoid issues by calling the opposition derogatory names. For example, during an environmental dispute, one side charged that its opponents were "little old ladies in tennis shoes" and "outside agitators." Not to be outdone, the other side labeled

ad hominem fallacy An attempt to discredit a position by attacking the people who favor it.

their antagonists as "rapists of public parkland."[34] Senator Zell Miller recently laced into *New York Times* columnist Maureen Dowd, a major critic of the Bush administration and of the religious right, in the following way: "The more Maureen Loud [sic] gets on 'Meet the Press' and writes those columns, the redder these states get. I mean, they don't want some highbrow hussy from New York City explaining to them that they're idiots and telling them that they're stupid." Miller also suggested "that red-headed woman at the *New York Times*" should not mock anyone's religion: "You can see horns just sprouting up through that Technicolor hair." Dowd responded: "I'm not a highbrow hussy from New York. I'm a highbrow hussy from Washington. Senator, pistols or swords?"[35] Presumably, the public was not much enlightened by this exchange.

Proof by ethos also can be abused when speakers overuse it—when they try to intimidate listeners by citing an overwhelming list of authorities while neglecting to present information or good reasons for accepting their claims.

Finally, speakers neglect their responsibility to prove their points when they merely assert what they have not proved, thereby **begging the question**. Those who beg the question usually rely on colorful language to disguise the inadequacy of their proofs so that the words themselves *seem* to establish the conclusion. Critics who shout, "It's amazing how much money we're wasting on education these days" suggest wild and excessive spending without really proving the allegation. A similar abuse may occur when the speaker taps into the mythos of the audience without adequate justification or preparation. A conclusion such as "Be *patriotic*! Support the *American way of life*! Speak out against gun control!"—tacked onto a speech without further explanation—begs the question, because the speaker has not proved that being against gun control is a form of patriotism.

Defective Patterns of Reasoning

Major fallacies may infest the basic patterns of reasoning in persuasion. It is unethical to commit them purposely, irresponsible to commit them accidentally. In your role as critical listener, be on guard against them at all times.

Errors of Reasoning from Principle. Reasoning from principle can be only as good as the underlying premise on which it is built. In the **shaky principle fallacy**, the premise is not sound. *If the principle is faulty, the entire argument may crumble.* We once heard a student begin a line of argument with the following statement of principle: "College athletes are not really here to learn." She was instantly in trouble. When her speech was over, the class assailed her with questions: How did she define *athletes*? Was she talking about intercollegiate or intramural athletes? How about the tennis team? How did she define learning? Was she aware of the negative stereotype at the center of her premise? Wasn't she being unfair, not to mention arrogant? It's safe to say that the speaker did not persuade many people that day. To avoid such a fiasco, be sure that you can defend each word in the principle that underlies your reasoning.

Omitted qualifiers, another fallacy common to reasoning from principle, occur when a persuader claims too much, in effect confusing probability with certainty. The logic of everyday life is rarely certain. Suppose a friend from the Tau Beta fraternity calls you to set up a blind date. If the principle "Tau Betas are handsome" holds about 90 percent of the time in your experience, and if you are

---

begging the question Assuming that an argument has been proved without actually presenting the evidence.

shaky principle fallacy A reasoning error that occurs when an argument is based on a faulty premise.

omitted qualifiers A reasoning error that occurs when a persuader claims too much, confusing probability with certainty.

about 90 percent certain that your blind date is a Tau Beta, then your conclusion that your date will be attractive is an assumption qualified by at least two factors of uncertainty. It is better to say: "There is a *good chance* that my date will be handsome." If you point out the uncertainty factor in advance through proper qualification, you may not lose the audience's trust if a prediction does not come true.

Errors of Reasoning from Reality.

An error common to reasoning from reality is *assuming that if something happens after an event, it was caused by the event.* This **post hoc fallacy** confuses association with causation. It is the basis of many superstitious beliefs. The same people who wear their lucky boots and shirts to ball games may also argue that we should have a tax cut because the last time we had one we avoided war, increased employment, or reduced crime. One of our students fell into the post hoc trap when she argued that low readership of certain books in areas where the books are banned in public schools proves that the bans are effective. There may be many reasons why people don't read books—banning them in school libraries may or may not be among those reasons. It is just as likely that the book bans themselves are simply symptoms of deeper cultural conditions and that the bans might actually create curiosity about their objects of censure, resulting in more readership than might otherwise have happened. A speaker must demonstrate that events are causally connected, not just make the assumption on the basis of association.

Another error common to such reasoning is a **hasty generalization** that is based on insufficient or nonrepresentative observations. Suppose a student reasoned, "My big sister in Alpha Chi got a D from Professor Osborn. The guy who sits next to me in history got an F from her. I'm struggling to make a C in her class. Therefore, Professor Osborn is a tough grader." To avoid hasty generalization, you would need to know what Professor Osborn's grade distribution looks like over an extended period of time and across courses, plus how her grades compare with other professors teaching the same courses.

Finally, an error common to both reasoning from principle and reasoning from reality is the **non sequitur fallacy**. It occurs when the principle and the reality discussed don't really relate to each other, when the conclusion does not follow from the relationship between them, or when the evidence presented is irrelevant. Former Speaker of the House Newt Gingrich, lecturing on why men are more suited than women to traditional military combat roles, provided a remarkable example that appears to fit all the conditions of non sequitur reasoning:

> If combat means living in a ditch, females have biological problems staying in a ditch for 30 days because they get infections. . . . [Moreover,] males are biologically driven to go out and hunt for giraffes.

Former Representative Pat Schroeder responded to this wisdom as follows: "I have been working in a male culture for a very long time, and I haven't met the first one who wants to go out and hunt a giraffe."[36]

And then there is the cockeyed non sequitur logic of the late Marge Schott, an owner of the Cincinnati Reds baseball team. Schott told a Denver radio audience that she would rather see children smoke than take drugs. Her reason? "We smoked a peace pipe with the Indians, right?"[37]

---

post hoc fallacy A deductive error in which one event is assumed to be the cause of another simply because the first preceded the second.

hasty generalization An error of inductive reasoning in which a claim is made based on insufficient or nonrepresentative information.

non sequitur fallacy A deductive error occurring when conclusions do not follow from the premises that precede them.

Defective Analogy. A **faulty analogy** occurs when the things compared are dissimilar in some important way. This fallacy lies at the heart of some of our most serious human problems. It rises out of our tendency to assume that what happened to us on one occasion is a sure indicator of what will happen to others in similar circumstances. A father reasons, "When I was a boy, my father made me work and it was good for me. Therefore, Junior should work." A mother answers, "When I was a girl my mother made me work and I hated every minute of it. Therefore, Junior should not work."

Which line of reasoning should win the argument? Neither. There are simply too many dissimilarities operating here. The times have changed, opportunities and expectations have changed, even the nature of the work may well have changed. And above all, neither Father nor Mother *is* Junior, who apparently has not been consulted.

Until they can expand their research to include many more case studies, enough to satisfy critical listeners, and are able to argue from more sound inductive grounds, these frustrated parents can offer only a clash of faulty arguments from analogy.

Fallacies Related to Particular Designs

In addition to fallacies of evidence, proof, and argument, there are at least two major fallacies related to particular persuasive designs. **Either-or thinking**, sometimes called a *false dilemma*, makes listeners think that they have only two mutually exclusive choices. This fallacy is attractive because it is dramatic: It satisfies our need for conflict and simplicity. It occurs in statements such as, "We can either promote jobs or protect the environment—not both" or "If we pay down the debt, we will sacrifice social security." Either-or thinking blinds listeners to other options, such as compromise or creative alternatives not yet considered. Such thinking often infests problem–solution speeches when speakers oversimplify the choices.

People with gardens sometimes make a "straw man" to scare off crows. As the name suggests, the straw is formed into the likeness of a man (presumably, a "straw woman" would work as well, as far as the crows are concerned). From this practice comes the **straw man fallacy**, creating a "likeness" of an opponent's view that makes it seem trivial, ridiculous, and easy to refute. As you might suspect, the straw man fallacy appears most often in speeches that contend with opposition. It understates and distorts the position of opponents and is unethical. Reducing the movement in favor of the Equal Rights Amendment for women to "an effort to abolish separate restrooms for men and women" or dismissing affirmative action as "a policy designed to give unfair advantage to minorities" are classic cases. As an ethical persuasive speaker, you have an obligation to represent an opposing position fairly and fully, even as you refute it. Only then will thoughtful listeners respect you and your arguments. The straw man fallacy is an implicit admission of weakness or desperation and can damage what may well be a legitimate case.

Persuasion is constantly threatened by flaws and deception. In a world of competing views, we often see human nature revealed in its petty as well as its finer moments. As you plan and present your arguments or listen to the arguments of others, be on guard against fallacies. Figure 15.6 lists and defines the fallacies we have been discussing.

---

faulty analogy A comparison drawn between things that are dissimilar in some important way.

either-or thinking A fallacy that occurs when a speaker suggests that there are only two options, and only one is desirable.

straw man fallacy Understating, distorting, or otherwise misrepresenting the position of opponents for ease of refutation.

Figure 15.6

Gallery of Fallacies

Kind	Nature of the Problem
1. Evidential fallacies	
A. Slippery slope	• Arguing that one bad thing will result in many others
B. Confusing fact with opinion	• Asserting opinions as though they were facts, or discrediting facts as opinions
C. Red herring	• Distracting listeners with sensational, irrelevant material
D. Myth of the mean	• Using an average to hide a problem
E. Flawed statistical comparisons	• Using percentage increases or decreases to distort reality
F. Defective testimony	• Omitting when a statement was made or a speaker's credentials; quoting out of context
G. Inappropriate evidence	• Using facts when examples are needed, or examples when facts are needed, or an intimidating list of authorities as a substitute for information
2. Flawed proofs	
A. Ad hominem	• Attacking the person rather than the point
B. Begging the question	• Assuming as decided what has actually not been proved
3. Defective arguments	
A. Shaky principle	• Basing an argument on an unsound assumption
B. Omitted qualifiers	• Confusing probability with certainty by asserting a conclusion without qualification
C. Post hoc	• Assuming because one event follows another, it was caused by it
D. Non sequitur	• Reasoning in which principles and observations are unrelated to each other or to the conclusion drawn
E. Hasty generalization	• Drawing conclusions based on insufficient or nonrepresentative observations
F. Faulty analogy	• Comparing things that are dissimilar in some important way
4. Persuasive design fallacies	
A. Either-or thinking	• Framing choices so that listeners think they have only two options
B. Straw man	• Belittling or trivializing arguments to refute them easily

In Summary

Persuasion is the art of getting others to consider our point of view fairly and favorably. In contrast with informative speaking, persuasive speaking urges a choice among options and asks for a commitment. Rather than speaking as a teacher, the speaker assumes the role of advocate. Ethical persuasive speaking centers on good reasons based on responsible knowledge. Persuasive speeches rely more on emotional involvement than do informative speeches, and they carry an even heavier ethical burden.

Argumentative Persuasion. Manipulative persuasion evades judgment and reflection by thoughtful listeners and avoids the ethical burden of justification. In contrast, argumentative persuasion displays the rationale for its conclusions in the form of evidence, proofs, and patterns of reasoning.

Developing Evidence and Proofs. When used in persuasion, supporting materials become evidence. Facts and statistics alert us to a situation we must change. Examples move listeners, creating a favorable emotional climate for the speaker's recommendations. Narratives bring a sense of reality and help listeners identify with the issue. Testimony calls on witnesses to support a position. When you use evidence, strive for recent facts and figures, emphasize factual examples, engage listeners through stories that make your point, and rely primarily on expert testimony.

Proofs constitute appeals to our rational nature (logos), appeals to feeling (pathos), appeals to the credibility of speaker and sources cited within the speech (ethos), and appeals to cultural identity (mythos). Appeals to rationality assume that we are thinking creatures who respond to well-reasoned demonstrations. Appeals to feeling affirm that we are also creatures of emotion. Appeals to credibility recognize that we respond to leadership qualities in speakers and to the authority of their sources of evidence. Appeals to cultural identity relate to our nature as social beings who respond to group traditions and values. Argumentative persuasion centers on the logos, but effective persuaders must be able to combine the strengths of these various forms.

Patterns of Reasoning. Persuaders must define the meanings of key terms and concepts early in their speeches. Definitions can also attempt to change

perspectives on subjects to make listeners more sympathetic to the arguments that will follow.

In deductive reasoning, speakers argue from accepted principles and values in order to justify their conclusions. Such reasoning originates in a principle (major premise), identifies some condition relevant to the principle (minor premise), and makes some judgment about the condition that seems justified by the principle (conclusion).

In inductive reasoning, speakers establish that their arguments are grounded in reality. Such reasoning from reality draws general conclusions from an inspection of particular related instances. It emphasizes evidence provided by facts, statistics, and expert testimony.

In analogical reasoning, persuaders show how we can deal with a problem by considering a similar situation. Such reasoning from parallel cases can help clarify an abstract problem by relating it to a more concrete model. The legitimacy of such reasoning depends on the adequacy of points of comparison.

Toulmin's model of argument displays how these patterns of reasoning can interact in public controversies.

Avoiding Defective Persuasion. Fallacies are errors in reasoning that can damage a persuasive speech. Evidence is defective when speakers misuse facts, statistics, and testimony. Common errors include the slippery slope fallacy, which assumes that a single instance will establish a trend; the confusion of fact with opinion; and the red herring, using irrelevant material to divert attention from the issue. Statistical fallacies include the myth of the mean, in which averages create illusions that hide reality, and faulty conclusions based on flawed statistical comparisons.

Various defects can reduce the value of proof. Speakers can commit an ad hominem fallacy, attacking the person rather than the argument. When speakers merely assume in their conclusion what they have not proved, they commit the fallacy of begging the question.

Fallacies are also common in the patterns of reasoning. If the principle you rely on is faulty, your entire argument will crumble. Or speakers can confuse association with causation, reasoning that if something happened after an event, it therefore was caused by the event. This is called the post hoc fallacy.

A non sequitur occurs when irrelevant conclusions or evidence are introduced into argument. Another error common to inductive reasoning is the hasty generalization, when conclusions are drawn from insufficient or nonrepresentative observations. Analogical reasoning is defective when important dissimilarities outweigh similarities.

Either-or thinking can be a special problem in speeches calling for action. This fallacy reduces audience options to only two, one advocated by the speaker, the other undesirable. When speeches that contend with opposition understate, distort, or misrepresent an opposing position for the sake of easy refutation, they commit the straw man fallacy.

Explore and Apply the Ideas in This Chapter

1. Examine magazine advertisements and newspaper articles to find "infomercials"—persuasive messages cloaked as information. What alerts you to the persuasive intent? In what respects does such communication possess the characteristics of persuasion and information discussed in this chapter?

2. Bring to class examples of advertisements that emphasize each of the four forms of persuasive proof: logos, pathos, ethos, and mythos. What factors in the product, medium of advertising, or intended audience might explain this emphasis in each example? Do the advertisements combine other forms of proof as well? How effective is each advertisement?

3. Analyze the evidence, proofs, and patterns of reasoning that develop in the speech by Bonnie Marshall, reprinted in Appendix B. How powerful is this overall design of persuasive materials? Might it have been even stronger? How?

4. Look for examples of fallacies in the letters-to-the-editor section of your local newspaper over a week's period of time. Bring these specimens to class for discussion and analysis.

5. Keep a diary for the next three days in which you identify all the moments in which you encounter

and practice persuasion. When were you most and least persuaded and most and least persuasive? Why? Did you encounter (or commit) any ethical abuses? Discuss your experiences in class.

6. Find a news story that interests you. Using the information in the story, (1) show how you might use this material as evidence in a persuasive speech, (2) indicate how this evidence might be used to develop a proof, and (3) explain how this proof might function as part of a pattern of reasoning.

7. About fifty years ago, in *The Ethics of Rhetoric*, Richard Weaver observed that frequent controversy over the definitions of basic terms in public discourse are a sign of social and cultural division.

   Look and listen for examples of lively disagreement over the definitions of the following terms in contemporary argument:

   a. preemptive war
   b. faith-based initiatives
   c. gun control
   d. same-sex marriage
   e. terrorism

   Do these disagreements reflect the kind of social division Weaver suggested?

The Secrets of Gun Violence in America
Richard F. Corlin

Dr. Richard Corlin, president of the American Medical Association, presented this controversial persuasive speech in 2001 at the AMA's annual meeting. The speech is a model of argumentative persuasion in that it emphasizes appeals to the reasoning capacity of listeners yet makes full use of what Aristotle described as "all the available means of persuasion."

. . . I grew up in East Orange, New Jersey, in the 1940s and 1950s. My high school was a mosaic of racial and ethnic diversity—equal numbers of blacks and whites, some Puerto Ricans, and a few Asians. We'd fight among ourselves from time to time [but] nobody pulled out a gun—none of us had them and no one even thought of having one. The worst wound anyone had after one of those fights was a split lip or a black eye.

. . . Back then, no parents in that town of mostly lower-middle class blue collar workers had to worry that their children might get shot at school, in the park or on the front stoop at home. But then again, that was also a time when we thought of a Columbine as a desert flower, not a high school in Littleton, Colorado.

. . . Today, it's very different. Guns are so available and violence so commonplace that some doctors now see gunshot wounds every week—if not every day. It's as if guns have replaced fists as the playground weapon of choice. The kids certainly think so. In a nationwide poll taken in March after two students were shot to death at Santana High School near San Diego, almost half of the 500 high school students surveyed said it wouldn't be difficult for them to get a gun. And one in five high school boys said they had carried a weapon to school in the last twelve months. One in five. Frightening, isn't it?

. . . With the preponderance of weapons these days, it comes as no surprise that gun violence—both self-inflicted and against others—is now a serious public health crisis. No one can avoid its brutal and ugly presence. No one. Not physicians. Not the public. And most certainly—not the politicians—no matter how much they might want to.

Let me tell you about part of the problem. In the 1990s, the CDC [Centers for Disease Control] had a system in place for collecting data about the results of gun violence. But Congress took away its funding, thanks to heavy lobbying by the anti–gun control groups. You see, the gun lobby doesn't want gun violence addressed as a public health issue. Because that data would define the very public health crisis that these powerful interests don't want acknowledged. And they fear that such evidence-based data could be used to gain support to stop the violence. Which, of course, means talking about guns and the deaths and injuries associated with them.

We all know that violence of every kind is a pervasive threat to our society. And the greatest risk factor associated with that violence—is access to firearms. Because—there's no doubt about it—guns make the violence more violent and deadlier.

Now my speech today is not a polemic. It is not an attack on the politics or the profits or the personalities associated with guns in our society. It isn't even about gun control. I want to talk to you about the public health crisis itself—and how we can work to address it, in the same way we have worked to address other public health crises such as polio, tobacco, and drunk driving.

In his opening Dr. Corlin builds ethos in a subtle way by suggesting that he came from humble beginnings. He also establishes a contrast between the more innocent past of his youth and the more dangerous present. This contrast sets up an important rhetorical move—his redefinition of gun violence as a "serious public health crisis."

Here Dr. Corlin establishes his agenda, his specific purpose. Because any speech bearing on firearms

401

in America must inescapably be contro-versial, he must also establish what are not his motives. He further defines a role for his lis-teners: As doctors, they are scientists, and they must approach this health crisis as scien-tists. In American soci-ety, science is a positive culturetype and scien-tists enjoy a positive symbolic identity as truth-seekers.

▶ *In this section, Dr. Corlin makes effective use of statistical evidence and inductive reasoning, consistent with his call for a scientific approach to the issue. He also uses comparison and contrast to highlight the power of the facts he introduces.*

▶ *In the sections that fol-low, Dr. Corlin may come close to contradicting his earlier promise not to deliver a polemic against the gun indus-try. And indeed, if gun violence is a serious health crisis, it's hard to see how he could avoid criticizing those who make guns so readily available and who resist efforts to regulate them.*

At the AMA, we acknowledged the epidemic of gun violence when—in 1987—our House of Delegates first set policy on firearms. The House recognized the irrefutable truth that "uncontrolled ownership and use of fire-arms, especially handguns, is a serious threat to the public's health inasmuch as the weapons are one of the main causes of intentional and unintentional injuries and death." In 1993 and 1994, we resolved that the AMA would, among other actions, "support scientific research and objective discussion aimed at identifying causes of and solu-tions to the crime and violence problem."

Scientific research and objective discussion because we as physicians are—first and foremost—scientists. We need to look at the science of the subject, the data, and—if you will—the micro-data, before we make a diagnosis. Not until then can we agree upon the prognosis or decide upon a course of treatment.

First, let's go straight to the science that we do know. How does this disease pres-ent itself? Since 1962, more than a million Americans have died in firearm suicides, homicides, and unintentional injuries. In 1998 alone, 30,708 Americans died by gunfire:

- 17,424 in firearm suicides

- 12,102 in firearm homicides

- 866 in unintentional shootings

Also in 1998, more than 64,000 people were treated in emergency rooms for nonfatal firearm injuries.

This is a uniquely American epidemic. In the same year that more than 30,000 people were killed by guns in America, the number in Germany was 1,164; in Canada, it was 1,034; in Australia, 391; in England and Wales, 211; and in Japan, the number for the entire year was 83.

Next, let's look at how the disease spreads, what is its vector, or delivery system. To do that, we need to look at the gun market today. Where the hard, cold reality is—guns are more deadly than ever. Gun manufacturers—in the pursuit of techno-logical innovation and profit—have steadily increased the lethality of firearms. The gun industry's need for new products and new models to stimulate markets that are already oversupplied with guns—has driven their push to innovate. Newer firearms mean more profits. With the American gun manufacturers producing more than 4.2 million new guns per year—and imports adding another 2.2 million annually—you'd think the market would be saturated.

But that's why they have to sell gun owners new guns for their collections—because guns rarely wear out. Hardly anyone here is driving their grandfather's 1952 Plymouth. But a lot of people probably have their grandfather's 1952 revolver. So gun manufacturers make guns that hold more rounds of ammunition, increase the power of that ammunition, and make guns smaller and easier to conceal.

These changes make guns better suited for crime, because they are easy to carry and more likely to kill or maim whether they are used intentionally or unintention-ally. In fact, one of the most popular handgun types today is the so-called "pocket rocket": a palm-sized gun that is easy to conceal, has a large capacity for ammuni-tion and comes in a high caliber.

The *Chicago Tribune* reported that the number of pocket rockets found at crime scenes nationwide almost tripled from 1995 to 1997. It was a pocket rocket in the hands of a self-proclaimed white supremacist that shot five children at the North Valley Jewish Community Center and killed a Filipino-American postal worker outside of Los Angeles in August of 1999.

Now, we don't regulate guns in America. We do regulate other dangerous products like cars and prescription drugs and tobacco and alcohol—but not guns. Gun sales information is not public. Gun manufacturers are exempt by federal law from the standard health and safety regulations that are applied to all other consumer products manufactured and sold in the United States.

No federal agency is allowed to exercise oversight over the gun industry to ensure consumer safety. In fact, no other consumer industry in the United States—not even the tobacco industry—has been allowed to so totally evade accountability for the harm their products cause to human beings. Just the gun industry.

In a similar pattern to the marketing of tobacco—which kills its best customers in the United States at a rate of 430,000 per year—the spread of gun-related injuries and death is especially tragic when it involves our children. Like young lungs and tar and nicotine—young minds are especially responsive to the deadliness of gun violence.

Lieutenant Colonel Dave Grossman, a West Point professor of psychology and military science, has documented how video games act as killing simulators, teaching our children not just to shoot—but to kill. Grossman, who calls himself an expert in "killology," cites as evidence the marksmanship of the two children, aged 11 and 13, in the Jonesboro, Arkansas, shootings in 1998. Both shooters were avid video game players. And just like in a video game—they fired off twenty-seven shots—and hit 15 people. Killing four of their fellow students—and a teacher. Such deadly accuracy is rare and hard to achieve—even by well-trained police and military marksmen.

I want you to imagine with me a computer game called "Puppy Shoot." In this game puppies run across the screen. Using a joystick, the game player aims a gun that shoots the puppies. The player is awarded one point for a flesh wound, three points for a body shot, and ten points for a head shot. Blood spurts out each time a puppy is hit—and brain tissue splatters all over whenever there's a head shot. The dead puppies pile up at the bottom of the screen. When the shooter gets to 1,000 points, he gets to exchange his pistol for an Uzi, and the point values go up.

If a game as disgusting as that were to be developed, every animal rights group in the country, along with a lot of other organizations, would protest, and there would be all sorts of attempts made to get the game taken off the market. Yet, if you just change puppies to people in the game I described, there are dozens of them already on the market—sold under such names as "Blood Bath," "Psycho Toxic," "Redneck Rampage," and "Soldier of Fortune." These games are not only doing a very good business—they are also supported by their own Web sites. Web sites that offer strategy tips, showing players how to get to hidden features like unlimited ammunition, access more weapons, and something called "first shot kill," which enables you to kill your opponent with a single shot.

We do not let the children who play these games drive because they are too young. We do not let them drink because they are too young. We do not let them smoke because they are too young. But we do let them be trained to be shooters at

Dr. Corlin's critique of the gun culture as it embeds itself in the lives of children is especially powerful. He uses authority and example to make his point and a striking analogy ("Puppy Shoot") to imprint it in the minds of listeners. His concrete and colorful language stimulates feeling as well as to thought, engaging pathos in the service of logos. Note in particular how his use of parallel construction magnifies the permissiveness of the gun culture.

an age when they have not yet developed their impulse control and have none of the maturity and discipline to safely use the weapons they are playing with. Perhaps worst of all, they do this in an environment in which violence has no consequences. These kids shoot people for an hour, turn off the computer—then go down for dinner and do their homework.

We need to teach our children from the beginning that violence does have consequences—serious consequences—all the time. Gunfire kills ten children a day in America. In fact, the United States leads the world in the rate at which its children die from firearms. The CDC recently analyzed firearm-related deaths in twenty-six countries for children under the age of fifteen—and found that 86 percent of all those deaths—occurred in the United States.

If this was a virus—or a defective car seat or an undercooked hamburger—killing our children, there would be a massive uproar within a week. Instead, our capacity to feel a sense of national shame has been diminished by the pervasiveness and numbing effect of all this violence. . . .

Having created a vivid ▶ *sense of the seriousness of the problem, Dr. Corlin turns to the question of action. What does he want listeners to do and not do? He calls for aggressive data collection concerning the issue, again making use of comparative statistics. He defines carefully the scope of such a research program, and uses argument by analogy—to the motor vehicle fatalities crisis—to suggest the feasibility and effectiveness of such research. He works to build listener confidence in the course of action he proposes.*

The question remains, what are we—the physician community—going to do about it? I can tell you first what we're not going to do. We're not going to advocate changing or abolishing the Second Amendment to the Constitution. . . . Our mission is not to abolish all guns from the hands of our fellow citizens. We're not advocating any limitations on hunting or the legitimate use of long guns, or for that matter, any other specific item of gun control. And we won't even be keeping a scorecard of legislative victories against guns in Congress and in the statehouses.

Why not? Because all these well-intentioned efforts have been tried by good people—and they have not met with success. Instead, they have been met with a well-organized, aggressive protest against their efforts by powerful lobbies in Washington and at the state and community levels. We—the American Medical Association—are going to take a different route—not just calls for advocacy—but for diplomacy and for statesmanship and for research as well. And make no mistake about this: We will not be co-opted by either the rhetoric or the agendas of the public policy "left" or "right" in this national debate about the safety and health of our citizens.

One of the ways we will do this is—to help assemble the data. Current, consistent, credible data are at the heart of epidemiology. What we don't know about violence—and guns—is literally killing us. And yet, very little is spent on researching gun-related injuries and deaths.

A recent study shows that for every year of life lost to heart disease, we spend $441 on research. For every year of life lost to cancer, we spend $794 on research. Yet for every year of life lost to gun violence, we spend only $31 on research—less than the cost of a taxi ride here from the airport.

That's bad public policy. It's bad fiscal policy. And it certainly is bad medical policy. If we are to fight this epidemic of violence, the Centers for Disease Control must have the budget and the authority to gather the data we need. As I mentioned earlier, the CDC's National Center for Injury Prevention and Control researched the causes and prevention of many kinds of injuries. But in the mid-90s the gun lobby targeted the NCIPC—and scored a bull's eye when Congress eliminated its funding. It wasn't a lot of money—just $2.6 million—budget dust to the federal government. But it meant the difference between existence and extinction for that project.

Just think—gun injuries cost our nation $2.3 billion dollars in medical costs each year—yet some people think $2.6 million dollars is too much to spend on tracking them. Every dollar spent on this research has the potential to reduce medical costs by $885.

The CDC is intent on doing its job and is now heading up the planning for a National Violent Death Reporting System—coordinated and funded at the federal level—and collecting data at the state level. Because knowing more about the who, what, when, where, why, and how of violent homicides, suicides, and deaths—will help public health officials, law enforcement, and policymakers prevent unnecessary deaths.

We must further insist that such a system be expanded to cover data about non-fatal gunshot injuries so that we can prevent these as well. Such a system of data collection and analysis has already helped us address another national epidemic—motor vehicle fatalities. Prompting preventive measures like mandatory seat belt laws, air bags, improved highway signage, and better designed entry and exit ramps—not the confiscation of cars. The establishment of a National Violent Death and Injury Reporting System would help us establish similar preventive measures against violence. And help us fill in all the blanks about violent death and injury in America. Including such basics as:

- How do kids with guns get their weapons?
- Do trigger locks work?
- What can we do to reduce accidental, self-inflicted gun injuries?
- What are the warning signs of workplace or school shootings?
- During which hours of the week and in what specific parts of town (down to individual blocks—not just neighborhoods) do the shootings occur?
- Do we need to work with police departments to change patrolling patterns based on these data?
- And finally, the realization that the answers to these questions are apt to be different from one town to the next.

Today, we can't answer these questions—because we are not allowed to collect the data. Collecting and considering the facts isn't a matter of opinion or politics, it's essential. It's a matter of working with other committed leaders to get the job done.

The good news is that we have HELP—the Handgun Epidemic Lowering Plan—with membership of 130 organizations including the AMA and, among others, the Rehabilitation Institute of Chicago, and the Minnesota Department of Health. We also have the Surgeon General's National Strategy for Suicide Prevention, released last month, which also supports the National Violent Death Reporting System.

We will not advocate any changes at all based on urban legend, anecdote or hunch. We will only base our conclusions on evidence-based data and facts. It's just good, common sense—the kind of solid epidemiology that has been brought to bear on other public health hazards—from Legionnaire's disease to food-borne illnesses to exposure to dioxin or DDT. Trustworthy science that can help us prevent harm before it happens. For, as we physicians know, prevention is usually the best cure.

One of the giants of American medicine, Dr. William Osler, proposed using preventive medicine against serious public health threats like malaria and yellow fever. And the tools he advocated—education, organization, and cooperation—sound like a pretty good definition of diplomacy to me. We will put these same tools to use in removing the threat of gun violence from our society.

As we have in the past, we have already sought the cooperation of the American Bar Association—and we are grateful that our invitation has been accepted. We will be working with the ABA on their Forum on Justice Improvements, taking place this October in Washington, D.C. The forum, set up by their Justice Initiatives Group, will focus on gun violence.

We are being advised by a panel of physicians and other experts, who have worked long and hard in tackling the many-headed monster of gun violence and its grisly outcomes. They have welcomed our involvement in this issue and look forward to a newly configured playing field with allies that command such clout as the ABA and the AMA.

Dr. Corlin acknowledges the risks of his program for action but appeals to the morality of his listeners and to the mythos of their organization. As doctors, they are obligated to help their patients overcome illness, in this case, the epidemic of gun violence. He suggests even that this may be a divine mission. His listeners can use this sacred principle as the deductive premise, the warrant, that justifies their acceptance of his proposal.

People have told me that this is a dangerous path to follow. That I am crazy to do it. That I am putting our organization in jeopardy. They say we'll lose members. They say we'll be the target of smear campaigns. They say that the most extremist of the gun supporters will seek to destroy us. But I believe that this is a battle we cannot not take on.

While there are indeed risks—the far greater risk for the health of the public, for us in this room, and for the AMA, is to do nothing. We, as physicians, and as the American Medical Association, have an ethical and moral responsibility to do this—as our mission statement says—"to promote the science and art of medicine and the betterment of public health." If removing the scourge of gun violence isn't bettering the public health—what is?

As physicians, we are accustomed to doing what is right for our patients—and not worrying about our comfort, ease or popularity. Our goal is to help cure an epidemic, not to win a victory over some real or imagined political enemy. Anyone who helps us in this fight is an ally—anyone.

We don't pretend to have all the answers. Nor do we expect the solution to be quick—and we certainly don't expect it to be easy. In fact, I am certain that we will not reach the solution during my term as your president. But, together as the American Medical Association—guided by our stated mission—we recognize our obligation to contribute our voice, our effort, and our moral imperative to this battle. And we will.

Almost a century ago, in his book *Confessio Medici*, Stephen Paget, the British physician and author, referred to medicine as a divine vocation. This is part of what he said:

"Every year young people enter the medical profession . . . and they stick to it . . . not only from necessity, but from pride, honor, and conviction. And Heaven, sooner or later, lets them know what it thinks of them. This information comes quite as a surprise to them . . . that they were indeed called to be doctors. . . . Surely a diploma . . . obtained by hard work . . . cannot be a summons from Heaven. But it may be. For, if a doctor's life may not be a divine vocation, then no life is a vocation, and nothing is divine."

We are here today as the guardians of that divine vocation and as such are dedicated to do what is right, whether or not it is comfortable, whether or not it is easy, and whether or not it is popular. Stephen Paget, you can rest well tonight. Your divine vocation is in good hands. We will guard it well. We will live up to our mission—we will do what is right.

Thank you.

Index

Note: *f* indicates figures.

Photo Credits

Chapter 1: Page 2: Kayte M. Deioma / PhotoEdit; 6: Bob Daemmrich/The Image Works; 8: Jonathan Nourok / PhotoEdit; 9: Alinari; 14: Jacobs Stock Photography/Getty Images; 20: Ryan McVay/Getty Images; **Chapter 2:** Page 24: Jupiter Images; 27: Gary Newkirk/NewSport/Corbis; 28: Chuck Savage/Corbis; 33: Tony Freeman/PhotoEdit; 39: Patrik Giardino/Corbis; **Chapter 3:** Page 44: Barbara Stitzer/PhotoEdit; 49: David Pu'u/Corbis; 50: Courtesy Beth Tidmore; 51: Alex Wong/Getty Images; 59: Bob Daemmrich/Stock Boston; 60: Terry Wild Studio; **Chapter 4:** Page 70: Stockbyte/Getty Images; 73T: Loren Santow; 73B: Lawrence Migdale, www.migdale.com; 76: Deborah Lerme Goodman; 80: Michael Newman/PhotoEdit; 85: Erik Freeland; **Chapter 5:** Page 94: AP/Wide World Photos; 98: Bob Daemmrich/The Image Works; 100: AP/Wide World Photos; 106: Blaine Harrington III/Corbis; 113: Michael Appleton/Corbis; 116: Christy Bowe/Corbis; **Chapter 6:** Page 120: Warren Morgan/Corbis; 123: Joel W. Rogers/Corbis; 131: Jeff Greenberg/The Image Works; 137: Photodisc/Getty Images; **Chapter 7:** Page 142: David Young-Wolff/PhotoEdit; 147: Rob Crandall; 149: Courtesy Google; 152: Courtesy Sierra Club; 153: Courtesy Mayo Clinic; 154: Colin Young-Wolff / PhotoEdit; 160: Ghislain & Marie David de Lossy/Getty Images; 163: Imagesource/Jupiter Images; **Chapter 8:** Page 168: © Paul Andrew Lawrence / Alamy; 172: Corbis; 176: NewSport/Corbis; 178: Scott Wintrow/Getty Images Sport; 185: AP/Wide World Photos; **Chapter 9:** Page 194: © Rachel Epstein / The Image Works; 198: Gary Connor/PhotoEdit; 202: Charles Gupton/Stock Boston; 207: Asahi Shimbun; 211: AP/Wide World Photos; 214: AP/Wide World Photos; 217: Kayte M. Deioma / PhotoEdit; **Chapter 10:** Page 222: Stuart Dee/Getty Images; 232: Frank Clarkson/Getty Images; 243: Getty Images; **Chapter 11:** Page 246: Junko Kimura/Getty Images; 249: AP/Wide World Photos; 253: Michael Newman/PhotoEdit; 260L: Michael Busselle/Corbis; 260R: AP/Wide World Photos; 261: Bosler Visual Works; **Chapter 12:** Page 282: Jim Hollander/epa/Corbis; 286: Hulton-Deutsch Collection Corbis; 290: AP/Wide World Photos; 300: Jeff Greenberg/PhotoEdit; 301: © Flip Schulke/Corbis; **Chapter 13:** Page 310: AP/Wide World Photos; 314: Joel Gordon 1993; 323: Courtesy Tom Osborn; 324: AP/Wide World Photos; 326: AP/Wide World Photos; 328: Reuters/Corbis; 332: Ghislain & Marie David de Lossy/Getty Images; **Chapter 14:** Page 340: Stan Honda/Getty Images; 345: © James Caldwell / Alamy; 349: Steve Rubin/The Image Works; 353: Fabrice Coffrini/Getty Images; **Chapter 15:** Page 368: AP/Wide World Photos; 372: Frederick Brown/Getty Images; 376: AP/Wide World Photos; 378: Rick Friedman/Corbis; 380: *American Progress*, John Gast, oil on canvas, 1987. Museum of the American West collection, Autry National Center; 383: AP/Wide World Photos; 392: Stockbyte/Getty Images; **Chapter 16:** Page 408: © Janusz Wrobel / Alamy; 412: Charles Gupton/Corbis; 414: Barry Rosenthal/Getty Images; 418: Bob Daemmrich/The Image Works; 422: Peter Turnley/Corbis; **Chapter 17:** Page 438: © Richard B. Levine; 443L: James Burke/Getty Images; 443R: Hulton-Deutsch Collection/Corbis; 446T: Alan Goldstein/Folio; 446B: © 2001 The Record (Bergen County, NJ); 448: AP/Wide World Photos; 449: Stewart Cohen/Getty Images; 456: AP/Wide World Photos